MORRIS AUTOMATED INFORMATION NETWORK
0 1029 0384521 6

W9-BNB-254

Franz Kafka

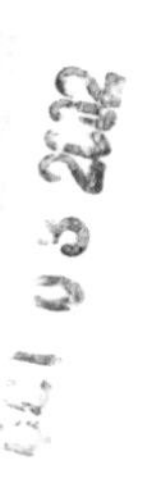

PARSIPPANY - TROY HILLS
PUBLIC LIBRARY SYSTEM

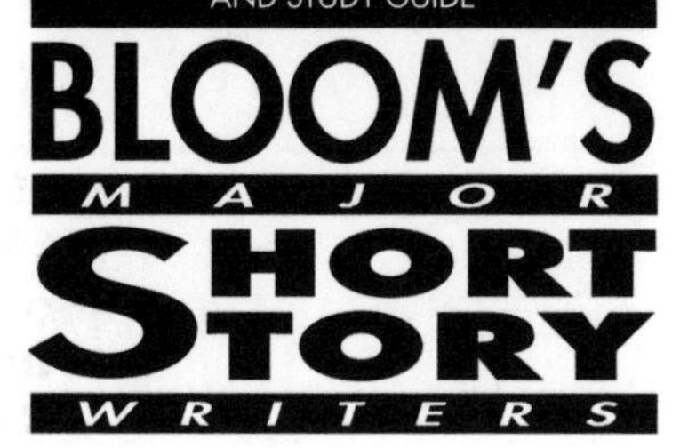

Franz Kafka

EDITED AND WITH AN INTRODUCTION BY HAROLD BLOOM

CURRENTLY AVAILABLE

BLOOM'S MAJOR DRAMATISTS

Aeschylus
Aristophanes
Bertolt Brecht
Anton Chekhov
Henrik Ibsen
Ben Johnson
Christopher Marlowe
Arthur Miller
Eugene O'Neill
Shakespeare's Comedies
Shakespeare's Histories
Shakespeare's Romances
Shakespeare's Tragedies
George Bernard Shaw
Neil Simon
Oscar Wilde
Tennessee Williams
August Wilson

BLOOM'S MAJOR NOVELISTS

Jane Austen
The Brontës
Willa Cather
Stephen Crane
Charles Dickens
William Faulkner
F. Scott Fitzgerald
Nathaniel Hawthorne
Ernest Hemingway
Henry James
James Joyce
D. H. Lawrence
Toni Morrison
John Steinbeck
Stendhal
Leo Tolstoy
Mark Twain
Alice Walker
Edith Wharton
Virginia Woolf

BLOOM'S MAJOR POETS

Maya Angelou
Elizabeth Bishop
William Blake
Gwendolyn Brooks
Robert Browning
Geoffrey Chaucer
Sameul Taylor Coleridge
Dante
Emily Dickinson
John Donne
H.D.
T. S. Eliot
Robert Frost
Seamus Heaney
Homer
Langston Hughes
John Keats
John Milton
Sylvia Plath
Edgar Allan Poe
Poets of World War I
Shakespeare's Poems & Sonnets
Percy Shelley
Alfred, Lord Tennyson
Walt Whitman
William Carlos Williams
William Wordsworth
William Butler Yeats

BLOOM'S MAJOR SHORT STORY WRITERS

Jorge Luis Borges
Italo Calvino
Raymond Carver
Anton Chekhov
Joseph Conrad
Stephen Crane
William Faulkner
F. Scott Fitzgerald
Nathaniel Hawthorne
Ernest Hemingway
O. Henry
Shirley Jackson
Henry James
James Joyce
Franz Kafka
D.H. Lawrence
Jack London
Thomas Mann
Herman Melville
Flannery O'Connor
Edgar Allan Poe
Katherine Anne Porter
J. D. Salinger
John Steinbeck
Mark Twain
John Updike
Eudora Welty

COMPREHENSIVE RESEARCH AND STUDY GUIDE

BLOOM'S MAJOR SHORT STORY WRITERS

Franz Kafka

Printed and bound in the United States of America.

First Printing
1 3 5 7 9 8 6 4 2

Library of Congress Cataloging-in-Publication Data

Bloom, Harold.
Franz Kafka / Harold Bloom.
p. cm. —(Bloom's major short story writers)
Includes bibliographical references and index.
ISBN 0-7910-6822-6
1.Kafka, Franz, 1883–1924—Criticism and interpretation. I.
Title.
II. Series.
PT2621.A26 B56 2002
833'.912—dc21

2002002776

Chelsea House Publishers
1974 Sproul Road, Suite 400
Broomall, PA 19008-0914

The Chelsea House World Wide Web address is http://www.chelseahouse.com

Contributing Editor: Dave Kress

Layout by EJB Publishing Services

CONTENTS

PLOT SUMMARY OF

"The Metamorphosis"

One of the strangest works of fiction of the Twentieth Century, this long story begins with an image that is at once chilling, foreboding, and comic—that is to say, pure Kafka: "As Gregor Samsa awoke one morning from uneasy dreams he found himself transformed in his bed into a gigantic insect." Accepting this horrifying change with a incongruous mixture of disbelief, discomfort, and resignation, Gregor matter of factly mulls over his demeaning and demanding job as a travelling salesman and tries to get back to sleep. But as the clock ticks on and Gregor finds himself later and later for a train he was supposed to have already caught, the rest of his family—his father, mother and younger sister, Grete—become increasingly anxious about him.

First his mother, then his father, and finally his sister ask after him, but as he tries to answer their questions to the best of his ability, he realizes he has practically lost his human voice as well as his human form: instead of words he produces only an odd insect buzzing.

Deciding that the best thing to do is simply get up and catch the later train, Gregor discovers that even getting out of bed now nearly impossible for him: multiple small legs of his insect body are seemingly beyond his control, and any movement is both difficult and painful. After several attempts at moving fail, Gregor remains in bed and listens through the walls as the chief clerk from the office arrives to inquire about Gregor's tardiness.

At first somewhat polite and concerned-sounding, the clerk at once begins to berate Gregor, accusing him through his locked door of laziness, ineptitude, and even embezzlement, and threatening to report him to their chief if he doesn't at once explain his refusal to show himself. One of the reasons that Gregor has taken this job is that his father owes the chief considerable money, and fearing that his family will suffer more than he will if he loses his job, Gregor attempts to reassure the clerk from inside his room. But by this time he cannot make any human sounds, and his insect chatter only terrifies his listeners and makes the whole situation unbearable.

In the outer rooms, Gregor's family and the clerk are shocked by the inhuman sounds Gregor is making, and the daughter and a servant girl are sent out in search of both a doctor and a locksmith. This action greatly relieves Gregor who feels himself, alien as he has become from family, work, and society, being somewhat drawn back into a circle of humanity. Encouraged by the aid his family is trying to provide, he tries to unlock the bedroom door himself; he succeeds by turning the key with his jaw, but he also hurts himself in the process—the first of many wounds he will begin to suffer as an insect. Finally opening the door, Gregor crawls into the living room, at last revealing himself to the astonished onlookers: the clerk gasps in shock and disgust, Gregor's mother screams and faints, and his father begins to weep uncontrollably.

Gregor tries to tell the clerk that he is about to go to work, and he begs the clerk for some understanding and sympathy for his present condition, but the clerk is so horrified that he begins to back out of the apartment in revulsion. Gregor moves to stop him, realizing that this is his last chance to explain the situation and win the clerk over to his side. He finds that for the first time that day he can move with no pain or effort, but Gregor's attempt to block the clerk's exit so thoroughly unnerves the clerk that he bolts from the apartment, screaming in fear and falling down the stairs. Gregor's mother again screams, knocking over the breakfast table, and his father, outraged by this, shoos Gregor back into his room and slams the door shut on him.

After falling into a swoon, Gregor awakens late in the afternoon as the sun is setting. Feeling even hungrier than he had earlier that day, Gregor is delighted to see that someone has been in his room and has left him a bowl of milk—his favorite food. But now he finds that fresh milk disgusts him and he cannot drink even a sip. It appears that his sister is the only one brave enough to enter the room, but also seeing how his appearance terrifies her, he takes to hiding under the sofa when she comes in, to make her short visits more palatable. She sees that he has left the milk untouched, and she surprises Gregor when she returns with a variety of foods, some wholesome and some rotten, to discover what now appeals to him. Out of all the things she brings him, he finds the most appealing is a piece of rotten cheese, and he greedily sucks it down. Although he is now at all. Even the garbage and trash cans are left there, as if the room were nothing more than a vacant storage room. Almost entirely forgotten by the family, Gregor finds that the only one who seems to notice him at all is the charwoman. For some reason unafraid of the giant insect, she boldly enters his room while he cowers in the corner form her taunts.

By this time, Gregor eats nothing at all, but as he listens to the lodgers eating their meals, he realizes that he is in fact starving—but for what exactly, he doesn't know. Having lost interest in almost everything human, Gregor is nevertheless drawn into the living room one evening—trailing dust, debris, and garbage form his body—by the sound of his sister's violin playing. At first no one notices Gregor. The lodgers, apparently finding that the sister's music does not meet their tastes, have moved to the window, impatiently waiting for the performance to end. They see Gregor there on the floor and are at first amused by his appearance. As the father tries to get them back into their room, though, they become angry and inform the father that they are giving notice and will not pay for the time they have spent there.

Grete rises to her feet and tells the mother and father that they have to get rid of this creature. She says what they all suspect and feel: that this insect cannot be Gregor, for if it were, he would have already left of his own accord and not stayed around to torment them and dishonor Gregor's memory. Limping back to his room, Gregor is finally exhausted and finds he cannot move at all. Realizing that his sister is right, and feeling he must leave even more powerfully than she does, Gregor is filled with feelings of love for his whole family—and in that moment he dies.

It is the charwoman who discovers the dead body the next morning, and when she informs the family they seem both mournful and relieved. The family now comes together more strongly than before, and with absolute authority, Mr. Samsa orders the lodgers out the apartment at once. The charwoman informs them that the "thing" has been taken care of, and feeling shaken but relieved, the family takes a day off from work and journeys to the country. It is early spring and the day is warm and sunny. Realizing that their prospects for the future are equally sunny, the two parents gaze at their daughter and the fine young woman she has become.

LIST OF CHARACTERS IN

"The Metamorphosis"

Gregor Samsa is a young man who works as a travelling salesman for an undisclosed business: a job and lifestyle he hates, but one he must continue with until his father's debts are paid off. Trapped between feelings of guilt and responsibility, Gregor finds his personal freedom corralled by both a demeaning job and a society that seems to dictate obedience. Thus Gregor is perhaps, already before the metamorphosis of the title, the quintessential alienated man: cut off from family, society, and eventually himself by a world in which he is not able to even know what "he himself" is or could do. In this way, Gregor's horrible transformation only gives visible and tangible proof of something that he has already become.

Gregor's younger sister, **Grete**, undergoes a positive metamorphosis almost the equal of Gregor's negative one—and is perhaps the actual subject of the story's title. At first a loving but almost spoiled and lazy girl, Grete is the only one who can brave the terror of Gregor's room. She tries to help him however she can with both food and by cleaning his room—but as time progresses, she begins to change. After she takes on a job to help out with the family's expenses, she begins to mature. By the end of the story she is the one who demands that the insect be gotten rid of; she is also the strongest family member at the end of the story, literally stretching herself both spiritually and physically.

Mr. Samsa, Gregor's father, also undergoes a metamorphosis in the story. When we first see him, he is a tired, fat old man who has been brought low by the failure of his business and by the transformation of his son. But once he takes on a job, lowly as it is, he finds new strength and authority, and by the end of the story he is starting to find new enjoyment in the world.

Gregor's mother, **Mrs. Samsa**, is perhaps the least developed character it the story. Mainly a worrier and a fainter, she wavers comically between devotion to her son and revulsion at what he has become: as all mothers do, perhaps? Though mainly in the background, she does tell us something about Gregor that might contradict his own perception of himself: he lives only for his job.

CRITICAL VIEWS ON

"The Metamorphosis"

Michael P. Ryan on the Influence of Eastern Philosophy

[Michael P. Ryan is a doctorate student and Fulbright scholar at The University of Pennsylvania whose primary interests include 20th-century literature as well as late 19th-century philosophy. Here, he interprets the story in terms of the influence of eastern philosophy on Kafka, especially in the connection between the name "Samsa" and the Sanskrit word "samsara."]

Franz Kafka was probably not a Hindu or Buddhist; however it does appear that he took an interest in their beliefs. One might consider, too, that it is not Samson or *sam jesm*, but *Samsara* that appears to connect all three of the stories within the *Strafen* ("Das Urteil," "Die Verwandlung," and "In der Strafkolonie"; Kafka, Briefe 147). Kafka tells Gustav Janouch, "words must be exactly and strictly defined... otherwise we may fall into entirely unexpected pitfalls" (Janouch 145). It has been suggested that Georg Bendemann (again the *mann* appears only to strengthen *Bende*), is perhaps derived from *Bande* (bonds, shackles, fetters). Here one might note the connection with *Samsara*'s translation as bondage. This could be the bondage of Kafka's relationship with his father, and the bondage of metempsychosis. In "Die Verwandlung," Gregor Samsa is a *Reisender*, a traveling salesman, which gives us *Samsara*'s second translation as "journey." *Der Reisende*, the main character in "In der Strafkolonie," completes the connection. These three stories may not be separate; they could be viewed as the chapters of one story; shackled together by the concept of metempsychosis. We might even call them "Kafkaesque," in the sense that Kafka is observing himself in various forms, always trying to escape his father. Hence, *Verwandlung* and its etymological connection with the third literal translation of *Samsara*—"*wandern*." *Samsara* serves the spirit of Kafka's writing, and this spirit is one of evasion, even deceit; Kafka intends for his works to be illusory. He alone stands as the exception to the elusiveness of his writing; it is *his* "escape" (Brod 25), and, playing the role of a fugitive, it is therefore fitting that only he, at the time of conception, knows the tunnels by which he absconds.

—Michael P. Ryan, "Samsa and Samsara: Suffering, Death, and Rebirth in 'The Metamorphosis'." *German Quarterly* 72 (1999): pp. 132-152.

Mark Sanders on the Ethical Implications of Gregor's Marginalization

[Mark Sanders is an assistant professor of English at Brandeis University. He is also the author of *Afro-Modernist Aesthetics and the Poetry of Stanley A. Brown* and *Complicities: The Intellectual and Apartheid and Ambiguities of Witnessing: On Testimony and Truth*. In this essay, Sanders argues that Kafka explores the marginality of Gregor Samsa in order to make an ethical and political critique.]

What is it like to be a bug? My question alludes to Thomas Nagel's famous essay on the philosophy of mind, "What is it like to be a bat?" (*Mortal Questions* 165–180). Nagel instills in us a healthy epistemological skepticism about representing animal and human others. Read along with a thinking of marginality drawn from cultural studies, *The Metamorphosis* helps us to see that, when it is a matter of representation, knowledge is only one part of the ethico-political puzzle. What matters is not simply what can or cannot be known about others, but how knowledge, or non-knowledge disguised as knowledge, is put into practice. (. . .)

The presentation of consciousness in Kafka's tale may be read as a commentary on the question posed by Nagel, and as an exploration of its bodily ramifications. *The Metamorphosis* opens with a fateful discovery: "When Gregor Samsa woke up one morning from unsettling dreams, he found himself changed in his bed into a monstrous vermin" ("zu einem ungeheuren Ungeziefer verwandelt") (3/93). The narrative begins by being focalized through Gregor by an impersonal third-person narrator. The narrative sequence places a doubly negative evaluation before Gregor's assessment of the details of his transformation. The narrator gives his chitinous condition a name before allowing him to register it in its particulars: the curved and vaulted back, the multitude of writhing legs, etc. The irony of the tale is that Gregor would appear to lose sight of the fact that to be an insect, or to be the insect that he has become, is also to be a "monstrous vermin" ("ein ungeheures Ungeziefer"). To be an insect is, however, not necessarily to be an *Ungeziefer*. When Vladimir Nabokov draws a sketch of Gregor as an inoffensive, albeit rather large, beetle (66), he allows one to imagine that there is nothing about his physical attributes and capacities to make him a "vermin." Nabokov's Gregor does not resemble insects typically classified as vermin such as lice or cockroaches. Yet the first sentence hangs over him like a portent as he acquaints himself with his insect-body and its powers, and as his sister Grete takes stock of his altered eating habits. In the end, however, Gregor's fate is sealed not by the information he and his sister collect, but by an act of naming performed by Grete which reiterates the tale's first sentence. The irony is that, although the first sentence appears to inform us that Gregor must be aware of his status, and must therefore anticipate his eventual destruction, he behaves as if he does not comprehend the implications of having the body he inhabits. Gregor adjusts to his insecthood by attending to his body, but does so as if oblivious that his new body is that of a creature liable to be treated as a "vermin." Curiously, most critics fail to take the mediation of Kafka's impersonal narrator into account. Reading the first sentence of the tale as simply a report of Gregor's waking thoughts, they assume an equivalence between insect and *Ungeziefer*. To do so is to not fully grasp Kafka's irony, which depends upon a play between narrator and focalizer, upon a play between Gregor's awareness of bodily alteration and its fatal naming.

—Mark Sanders, "What is it Like to be a Bug?: 'The Metamorphosis' and Marginality." *Journal of the Kafka Society of America* 20 (1996): pp. 55-58.

J. Brooks Bouson on the Metaphors of Narcissism

[J. Brooks Bouson is a professor of English at Loyola University of Chicago. His publications include *Quiet As It's Kept: Shame, Trauma, and Race in the Novels of Toni Morrison*. In this article, Bouson poses the idea that reading the story as an example of the psychology of self-awareness can reveal its analysis of an important narcissistic drama.]

In the black comedy of his initial confrontation with the office manager and his family, Gregor satisfies his desire for attention and his grandiose wish to exert magical power over others. For when he makes his first appearance as an insect, his father clenches his fist as if to strike, then falters and begins to sob; his mother collapses; the loathed office manager, obeying Gregor's unconscious wish to get rid of him, slowly backs out of the room, then, his right hand outstretched, approaches the staircase "as if nothing less than an unearthly deliverance were awaiting him there" (17), and finally flees. But Gregor's exhibitionistic display is short-lived. His traumatic rejection at the very moment he shows himself points to a central cause of his self-disorder as it repeats and telescopes his experience of early parental rejection and the long series of similar rejections he has suffered throughout his life, these rejections pivotal in the formation of his distorted self-image.

Just as his family turns away from him, so the reader, while encouraged to sympathize with Gregor, is at the same time prompted to shun him as the text insistently focuses attention on his physically repulsive insect's body. And while we are meant, as one critic has observed, to "respond to the plight of the loathly son" in this scene, it is also true that "our compassion and our understanding seem mocked by the opposing image of a man shooing away a bug." In part, this scene reads like some sort of "grotesque joke." (. . .)

What is so central to the self-drama of Gregor Samsa—the insect-Gregor's desperate need for attention—is also central to the reader's transactions with Kafka's hapless character. Indeed, from the very first sentence of *The Metamorphosis* and throughout the narrative, Kafka focuses the reader's attention on the insect-Gregor. The narrator, located both within and without Gregor's subjectivity, acts as an objective reporter of his plight and as an extension of his consciousness. While essentially confined to Gregor's perspective and drawn into his inner world, the reader is also positioned at a slight remove from him, this partial detachment serving to ward off potential reader anxieties about being enmeshed in his claustrophobic insect's world. Encouraged to experience a wide variety of emotional responses, ranging from disgust and physical revulsion to pity and a desire to see Kafka's antihero rescued, the reader, above all, is compelled to rivet attention on the insect-Gregor. Inscribed in *The Metamorphosis* is Gregor's protracted attempt to procure the notice of others so he can temporarily sustain his defective self.

—J. Brooks Bouson, "The Narcissistic Drama and the Reader/Text Transformation in Kafka's *Metamorphosis*." *Critical Essays on Franz Kafka*, by Ruth V. Gross, (Boston: G.K. Hall & Co, 1990): pp. 191-208.

Stanley Corngold on How Metaphor is Made Literal

[Stanley Corngold is a professor of German and Comparative Literature at Princeton University. He has written extensively on Kafka and is the author of *The Fate of the Self: German Writers and the French Theory and Franz Kafka: The Necessity of Form*. In this article, Corngold proposes that part of the reason the story ends so unsuccessfully has to do with how Kafka struggled to come to terms with its beginning.]

The distortion of the metaphor in *The Metamorphosis* is inspired by a radical aesthetic intention, which proceeds by destruction and results in creation—of a monster, virtually nameless, existing as an opaque sign. "The name alone, revealed through a natural death, not the living soul, vouches for that in man which is immortal"

(Adorno). But what is remarkable in *The Metamorphosis* is that "the immortal part" of the writer accomplishes itself odiously, in the quality of an indeterminacy sheerly negative. The exact sense of his intention is captured in the "*Ungeziefer*," a word which cannot be expressed by the English words "bug" or "vermin." *Ungeziefer* derives (as Kafka probably knew) from the late Middle High German word originally meaning "the unclean animal not suited for sacrifice." If for Kafka "writing is a form of prayer" (*Dearest Father*), this act of writing reflects its own hopelessness. As a distortion of the "genuine" names of things, without significance as a metaphor or as literal fact, the monster of *The Metamorphosis* is, like writing itself, a "fever" and a "despair."

The metamorphosis of a vermin-metaphor cannot be understood as a real vermin, as that biting and blood-sucking creature to which, for example, Kafka has his father compare him in his *Letter to His Father*. But it may be illuminated by the link which Kafka established earlier between the bug and the activity of writing itself. In the story "Wedding Preparations in the Country" (1907), of which only a fragment survives, Kafka conjures a hero, Eduard Raban, reluctant to take action in the world (he is supposed to go to the country to arrange his wedding); Raban dreams instead of autonomy, self-sufficiency, and omnipotence.

—Stanley Corngold, "Metamorphosis of the Metaphor." *Mosaic 3*, no. 4 (1970). Reprinted in Franz Kafka's "*The Metamorphosis*," ed. Harold Bloom, (New York: Chelsea House, 1988): p. 44.

Evelyn Tornton Beck on the Similarities Between Kafka's Story and Gordin's Play *The Savage One*.

[Evelyn Tornton Beck is a professor of Comparative Literature, German, and Women's Studies at the University of Wisconsin. She is the author of *Nice Jewish Girls: A Lesbian Anthology and Kafka and the Yiddish Theater: Its Impact on his Work*. In this article, Beck argues for the ways in which Kafka's tale can be elucidated by an understanding of an earlier work, a play by Gordin called *The Savage One*.]

Although one would never assert that the metamorphosis can be fully explained as a metaphor for Gregor's subservience within the family or on the job, nevertheless, in order for the narrative to cohere, one must assume that Gregor's animal shape embodies some essential aspect of his previous human experience. Kafka deliberately leaves the meaning of his central symbol partially obscure; Gordin, however, provides us with an explicit key to his work, which aids our understanding of the Kafka story as well. Near the end of the play Lemekh's brother explains: "What—where is this savage one? A savage who observes our behavior and our ways is buried deep within each of us. . . . When we improve ourselves, when the spirit in us wakens, when our souls reign over our bodies, then the savage one within us sleeps. But, when we strive only for material goals, when we have no ideals, when our spirit sleeps, then the savage one awakens and forces us to go against civilization, against the laws of humanity!" ("Vos? Vu iz der vilder mentsh? Der vilder mentsh zitst tif bagrobn bay yedn fun unz, betrakht alle unzer benemen, unzer oyffirung. . . . Ven mir bildn zikh, ven der gayst ervakht in unz, ven unzer zele hersht iber'n kerper, dan shloft in unz der vilder mentsh, ober farkert, ven vir shtrebn nur tsu matiriele tsiln, ven vir hobn kayne idealn, ven unzer gayst shloft, dan vakht in unz der vilder mentsh, velkher tsvingt unz tsu geyn gegn tsivilizatsion, gegn di gezetse der mentshhayt.") This analysis of one who would fall prey to the animal instinct within him perfectly describes Gregor as he is shown to have been before the metamorphosis: a man of few ideals, devoted single-mindedly to material gain. His mother unwittingly reveals the paucity of his previous existence: "The boy thinks about nothing but his work." ("Der Junge hat ja nichts im Kopf als das Geschaft.") Even the one ideal that Gregor seems to have lived for—his plan to send his sister to the music conservatory—is presented in terms of money ("despite the great expense that would entail, which must be made up in some other way"). ("Ohne Rücksicht auf die grossen Kosten, die das verursachen musste, und die man schon auf andere Weise hereinbringen würde.")

Gordin's play warns of the "beast" lurking in every man beneath the human facade. Similarly, Kafka seems to be pointing to the vermin which every man inherently embodies. While most readers will not be ready to accept Gregor as a universal symbol of man, it is difficult to escape the conclusion that in *The Metamorphosis* Kafka is portraying what was, at least at that time, his own despairing, tragicomic vision of the human condition.

—Evelyn Tornton Beck, "The Dramatic in Kafka's *The Metamorphosis*." *Kafka and the Yiddish Theater: Its Impact on His Work.* Reprinted in *Franz Kafka's "The Metamorphosis*." ed. Harold Bloom, (New York: Chelsea House, 1988): pp. 59–60.

PLOT SUMMARY OF

"The Judgement"

One Sunday morning in spring, a young merchant named Georg Bendemann finds his thoughts turning to a friend of his who had left years earlier to seek his fortune in Russia. The friend has not been home more than three years, and Georg wonders if he should write the friend to tell him of his own business success and recent engagement.

Georg is uncertain whether or not to write because the friend's own health and fortune have plummeted during his absence, and Georg does not want to make the friend feel worse about his own situation—or so it seems. Further complicating Georg's uncertainty is his relation with his father, from whom he has taken over the family business since Georg's mother died two years earlier. Georg has discussed these rather odd circumstances with his fiancée, Fraulein Frieda Brandenfield, who is troubled by Georg's relationship with his absent friend and urges him to write with the news of their approaching wedding.

In fact, it is revealed that Georg has already written the letter and is actually wondering whether or not to mail it. Unable to make up his mind, Georg crosses the hall to his father's room—which he has not been in for three months—to ask his father's advice. In a dark and shabby room, surrounded by mementos of his dead wife, the father sits alone, apparently reading a huge newspaper.

At first, the father claims to have no idea of what Georg is talking about and declares that he has no recollection of this friend at all. After Georg's lengthy explanations and prompts fail to jog the father's memory, Georg becomes concerned for his father's health. He lays the old man in bed, covering him up with heavy blankets. At this point, the old man leaps up in bed and—balancing with one hand on the ceiling—looking down at Georg, begins to berate him. The father states that he has been waiting years for Georg to come to him with just this quandary: he remembers the absent friend all too well, that Georg has in fact abandoned him for the wanton attention of Fraulein Brandenfield.

When Georg's mood suddenly turns sarcastic, his father reveals that he has been corresponding with the friend in Russia for years—and that the friend knows all about Georg's alleged success and his engagement. Bombarding Georg with guilt over how he has treated him and the friend, Georg's father further reveals that he has always considered the friend more of a son than Georg. Finally, the father passes the judgement of the story's title: he tells Georg that he is condemned to die by drowning. Feeling himself drawn from his father's room by a power he cannot resist, Georg dashes out of the building and through the busy streets to a bridge. He leaps over the railing but hangs on for just a moment: when the street sounds are sufficiently loud to drown out his fall, Georg lets go of the railing and falls into the river below.

LIST OF CHARACTERS IN

"The Judgement"

Georg Bendemann is a youngish businessman of indeterminate age who has taken over the family business from his father after the death two years earlier of his mother. An introspective man who seems locked in a pattern of hyper-logical inaction, Georg seems to be unable to take decisive action. He overanalyzes the question of what he should tell his friend about either the news of their town or of his impending marriage to his fiancée. Although he suffers terrible guilt for taking the business away from his father, and although his father also blames him for deserting his own friend, Georg is ultimately the good son: upon hearing his father's judgement, Georg himself carries out the sentence in a fashion that actually recalls his parents' earlier pride in him.

Georg's **father**, though unnamed, old, and weak in the story, comes to stand taller than Georg—and more powerful. Clown, judge, and tyrant rolled into one, he lies in wait for some sign of Georg's weakness, for some chance to pass judgement on his son's alleged misdeeds. After the death of his wife the father has retreated from the world and his business to the dark confines of his shabby room. Still a giant of a man in Georg's perception, the father teases, tests, and torments Georg, forcing Georg to literally execute himself for what are probably hallucinations on the father's part.

CRITICAL VIEWS ON

"The Judgement"

ALLEN THIHER ON THE SELF-REFERENTIAL ASPECTS

[Allen Thiher is a professor of French at the University of Missouri—Columbia. He is also the author of *Celine: The Novel as Delirium and Raymond Queneau*. This extract is taken form *Franz Kafka: A Study of the Short Fiction* and argues that "The Judgements" clearly shows Kafka as part of the postmodern tradition in which a text's references to itself are what construct a text and what allows us to construe it.]

Kafka begins the story by presenting an image of writing, for Georg sits mulling over the possibility of writing to a friend in Russia about Georg's forthcoming marriage or about his success in business. On one level this writing could be nothing more than the communication of a message, of information sent across a vast space. That space in a literal sense is the vast plains of Russia, though on reflection the reader may suspect that this is a space that, like the great expanse of China in later tales, no message could ever cross. Kafka starts the story, then, with a reference to the space of communication, or that space of infinite loss in which all messages go astray. Writing in this space of ironic reversals never really aims at an outer world, but only designates itself and the space within which it is enclosed. As the rest of the story makes clear, Georg's letter can never be mailed.

With this reference to writing at the story's beginning Kafka has inscribed within his text a double for what the reader takes to be a story's usual function. Like a letter, a story should transcend its own immanent space by performing referentially as a form of communication. This doubling is underscored when Georg, having finished the difficult task of writing the letter, continues to sit at the table: "With the letter in his hand, his face turned toward the window, Georg had remained seated at the table for a long time. As an acquaintance passed by and greeted him from the street, he had barely answered with an absent smile" (modified translation of p. 80). The image of the window here, as in the stories we have already discussed as well as in "The Metamorphosis" and *The Trial*, appears as an image of the desired transparency, of the opening onto the world that would allow the genesis of meaning and a communication opening out of the text. The constant play between inner and outer space in Kafka's settings often stands as an analogue for the relationship between the narrative space within language and an extratextual space beyond the closed labyrinth of the narration. Georg, the writer who has not completed his narration, seems to have trouble at this moment establishing a contact with some "exteriority" beyond the space that contains him. The passing acquaintance whom Georg scarcely acknowledges would, in this perspective, be another double in this network of doubles, in this case it would be a double for the friend in Russia to whom Georg's letter is addressed. And the absent smile is another sign of the absence that permeates this paradoxical text; it would be the ironic smile produced by the impossibility of making contact through the window that is often a barrier, not a source of illumination of Kafka's world.

—Allen Thiher, "The Judgement." *Franz Kafka: A Study of the Short Fiction*, (Boston: Twayne, 1990): pp. 33-50.

Stanley Corngold on the Figural Tension Between Georg and His Father

[In this essay, Corngold suggests that the narrative tension between Georg and his father is paralleled by a figural one in which the father's metaphorical expressions are combated with Georg's cantankerous literal ones.]

To the father's every figurative utterance, Georg responds with a crass literalizing, as if this could impose powerful constraints all in his favor on the necessarily figurative language of dialogue. Georg aims to deny the father the power to speak figuratively, the power to form sentences through the figurative stock of the language. To literalize his father's language is to reify him, seize and possess him. Theirs is a wild contest for the power to make metaphors. Says the father: "I have made a glorious alliance with your friend, I have your customers here in my pocket." Thinks Georg, literalizing: "He has pockets even in his shirt" and that with this comment "he [Georg] could make him [his father] an impossible figure for all the world." The father replies: "How you amused me today, coming to ask me if you should tell your friend about your engagement. . . . He knows everything a hundred times better than you do yourself. . . ." "Ten thousand times!" says Georg, taking the numerical point literally, "so as to make fun of his father, but in his very mouth the words took on a deadly sound."

—Stanley Corngold, "Kafka's 'The Judgement' and Modern Rhetorical Theory" *Newsletter of the Kafka Society of America* 7 no. 1 (1983): pp. 15-21.

JAMES M. MCGLATHERY ON KAFKA'S ANXIETY ABOUT HIS OWN MARRIAGE

[James M. McGlathery is a professor of German and of Comparative Literature at the University of Illinois at Urbana-Champaign. He is also the author of *E.T.A. Hoffman and Fairy Tale Romance: The Grimms, Basile, and Perrault.* In this piece, McGlathery argues that Kafka's tale shows us evidence of Kafka's own ironic and humorous panic at the prospect of marrying.]

Georg Bendemann's problem with his father, or more specifically, his inability to escape from his father's domination, would seem to be the point of "The Judgement." Despite his factual position as head of the family business, now that his father has retired following the mother's death, Georg continues to relate to his father emotionally as though he, Georg, were still a boy. Such feelings were a problem for Kafka himself, and critics have duly emphasized this aspect of the story. Yet the immediate issue facing Kafka at the time he wrote "The Judgement" was that variation of the Hamlet question as formulated, for example, by Oskar Matzerath in Grass' *Tin Drum*: "To marry or not to marry?" Georg Bendemann's tentativeness regarding marriage may, as some critics have suggested, be the product of a classic Oedipus complex. But unconscious sexual revulsion—a revulsion found consciously and candidly expressed in Kafka's diaries—may be even more basic to Georg's ambivalence regarding his approaching nuptials.

If "The Judgement" is read from this perspective, then Georg's nightmarish confrontation with his father over the contemplated change in his marital status, together with his speculations about his absent friend's likely reaction to the news of his engagement, may be nothing more than fantasies projecting Georg's own unconscious, irrational feelings of sexual guilt, panic, and revulsion. Most important, this view provides better and more sufficient cause for Georg's desperate, suicidal leap from the bridge at the end. Such compulsive, almost mechanical behavior is unlikely in the case of anyone who has faced and recognized his problem, and Georg does not seem to be in much doubt about the nature of his relationship to his father. What he may be suppressing instead is guilt and panic about the wedding night. In this case, the father's condemning him to death by drowning may be no more than a voice from within, projected onto the father in order that Georg will not have to admit to himself the true reason for his consequent need and urge to escape. Kafka, by contrast, was quite able to admit to himself not only his feelings toward his father, but also those regarding sex; otherwise Kafka might indeed have ended as a suicide, like George, and would not, in any case, have become a writer of such genius.

—James M. McGlathery, "Desire's Persecutions in Kafka's 'Judgement,' 'Metamorphosis,' and 'A Country Doctor'" *Perspectives on Contemporary Literature* 7 (1981): pp. 54-63.

Bluma Goldstein on the Relationship Between Economic Factors and Social Behavior

[Bluma Goldstein was a professor of German at University of California at Berkeley. She is the author of *Moses: Heine, Kafka, Freud, and Schoenberg in a European Wilderness*. In this article drawn from Flores, Goldstein contends that the interrelationships of the individual, the economy, and society as a whole constitute the problem or predicament for Georg in "The Judgement."]

"The Judgment" presents a complex of social problems as Georg Bendemann is confronted with a crisis in his relationship—with his father, friend, fiancée, indeed with his entire way of living. This crisis is not, as many critics have maintained, that of Everyman or Anyman standing on the threshold of adulthood, on the border between youth and maturity, license and responsibility, individuality and community; nor is it a crisis in expressing the ineluctable and unresolvable contradictions of human existence. Rather it is Georg Bendemann's predicament, and we may experience it as ours also; but if it is indeed ours, it is probably because we share experiences and an environment that are similar to his. Nor are Georg and his father every father and son, but very particular relatives in a specifically characterized environment. They are presented and confront each other in their home and are, in part, characterized by their place in it. In his bright, airy room the son stares through an open window at an expansive vista outside, while in a corner of his room at the rear of the house, the father sits surrounded by mementoes of his past life and of the wife who had died several years ago—it is stuffy, in disarray with old newspapers and the remains of an uneaten breakfast. The description of the contrasting rooms of son and father already suggests the character of the inhabitants: the externalized and unconnected young man and internalized father who cherishes deep commitments to people and to his past, is unconcerned with external elements—dirt, food, time. Careful details of their surroundings and poignant presentation of significant episodes—not description and definition of characters—reveal the quality of the character and personality. Thus, it is the relationships of characters with one another and with their environment that characterize the people. For example, just as Georg is leaving his room to visit his father, one single sentence discloses the quality of Georg's relationships, the distance and sterility; he turns toward the window—a frequent motif in Kafka's works that suggests the separation of people and environment as well as a strong sense of isolation and insulation of a person—"He had barely acknowledged, with an absent smile, a greeting waved to him from the street by a passing acquaintance" (*PC*, 54). Georg's remoteness here is accentuated by the following scene in the father's bedroom where the old man. surrounded by reminders of a life he had cherished, pursues the problem of the son's sociality.

Relationships are of prime importance in this story. Only in the character and quality of relationships do we learn anything about the figures themselves. Here people are precisely what their relationships are, and these include not only those with people, but with their work and their social environment. Thus, information about Georg is communicated through his relationships with father, friend, and fiancée, with his home, and with his business activity. Precisely because his character is intimately connected with his entire social life, insight into his general behavior elucidates not only the nature of his bachelor existence, but also the reasons for the crisis which culminates in the father's condemnation and the son's suicide.

—Bluma Goldstein, "Bachelors and Work: Social and Economic Conditions in 'The Judgement,' 'The Metamorphosis,' and *The Trial.*" *The Kafka Debate: New Perspectives for Our Time* edited by Angel Flores, (New York: Gordian: 1977): pp. 147-176.

V. Murrill and W.S. Marks III on the Connections Between Kafka's Story and Freud's Work on Dreams

[V. Murrill and W.S. Marks III were both professors at the University of California, Santa Barbara. In this essay, the two authors argue that Kafka's enigmatic story can be best understood as an attempt by Kafka to work out his own response to Freud's important work on dreams.]

The suggestion of a released sexual energy in the final paragraph (where Georg springs through the gate and, driven in the water, vaults over the bridge rail "like the distinguished acrobat he had been in his youth" to plunge beneath "an unending stream of traffic [Verkehr, also intercourse]") culminates with this concluding pun. Concerning the sexual associations connected with memories of being raised and lowered by playful parents, Freud remarks that older children love to repeat these delightful experiences in dreams, where "they leave out the hands which hold them up so that they float or fall unsupported..." As in the final paragraph of "The Judgment," the dreamer's death-defying and autonomous acrobatics express both the child's wish for freedom from the father and a primitive artistic impulse—Rank's "will-to-art." Neither stifled nor sublimated, sexuality is here consumed by a deeper desire. Emanating from the father, the force that propels Georg along his fatal course to the river is, in perhaps its largest sense, the power of the past. Among other reasons Kafka wrote "The Judgment" to propitiate this power and thus to master it. The ambiguity of the story's catastrophe (has Georg perished utterly or suffered a rebirth; have we a tragedy or a comedy?) bespeaks that imperviousness to analysis of both the dream and the act of magic. In both these activities, as in psychoanalysis, the gods are invoked that they may be more effectively dismissed; our bondage to them is affirmed so that our freedom from them may be better secured. Kafka seems to be resigning himself to this paradox in his last words on the story's personal meaning:

> What they [the Bendemanns] have in common is built up entirely around the father, Georg can feel it only as something foreign, something that has become independent, that he has never given enough protection, that is exposed to Russian revolutions, and only because he himself has lost everything except his awareness of the father does the judgment, which closes off his father from him completely, have so strong an effect on him.

We may have either God the Father or His divine justice, but not both. With this sentence Kafka finally separates the religious or communal life of the family from the moral life of the individual (and hence from the life of art). With "The Judgment" Kafka took his spiritual departure from the house of his father to join his fellow exile Dostoevsky—whom Freud too could call his "friend in St. Petersburg."

—V. Murrill and W.S. Marks III, "Kafka's 'The Judgement' and *The Interpretation of Dreams*." *The Germanic Review* 48 (1973): pp. 212-228.

PLOT SUMMARY OF

"In the Penal Colony"

One of Kafka's most disturbing and difficult tales, "In the Penal Colony" tells the story of an unnamed explorer who is asked to witness an execution. Taking place somewhere in the tropics in an undisclosed colony of an unknown nation, the story begins with the officer's assessment of the death machine: "It's a remarkable piece of apparatus." Though the story is told from the perspective of the third person, in reality the narrative is almost identical with the explorer and only occasionally delves into the inner consciousness of other characters.

The explorer is not very interested in the execution and in fact is only there out of obligation or politeness to the officer. The officer on the other hand, is thoroughly consumed with the machine itself as well as all of the preparations for setting it in order. While the explorer seems more interested in the terrain and topography of the colony, the officer cannot help but discuss the operation of the machine. Almost in the background, the prisoner—who has insulted his superior officer and has been condemned to death—waits stupidly and patiently for the execution to begin. After alluding to his devotion to the colony's former Commandant—with whom he worked on the death machine—the officer begins to explain how the machine itself works.

Briefly, the machine is designed to literally sentence the condemned to death: using sharp needles which etch deeper and deeper with repeated movements, it writes the actual death sentence on the prisoner's body. Since this particular prisoner is guilty of insubordination, the sentence of his death is one of the simple rules of the colony, "Honor thy superiors." The explorer learns also of the strange mode of justice on the island: prisoners are never informed of their crime, given a chance to defend themselves, nor told their punishment—until the machine begins working on their bodies. As the needles repeat the death sentence, the officer explains, the prisoner's own body tells him the sentence just as he dies. The entire execution normally takes a good twelve hours to complete, for at first the inscription causes only pain and discomfort.

But, as the officer explains, at the sixth hour the prisoner, completely weakened by loss of blood and wracked by pain, becomes enlightened: he begins to decipher the machine's embellished script through his own wounds. As the prisoner is laid on the machine, one of the wrist straps breaks, and while the officer rages against the intrigues of the new Commandant, the explorer finds himself wondering if he should intervene. Though normally only an observer, he feels so much terror at the implications of the execution that he begins to feel that it would be wrong to do nothing but watch. But just then the condemned man vomits as a felt gag is placed in his mouth, the explorer learns that in the past three months alone more than a hundred men have been killed on the machine. Further, the officer explains that he is the only member of the entire penal colony who still supports the use of the machine. The officer tells the explorer of the former grand days of the machine's use and of how far the entire execution ceremony has fallen from official favor. Further, the officer tells the explorer that he knows the explorer will be asked to report the results of the execution to the new Commandant, to judge, in effect, the officer himself. In the end, he begs the explorer to help against the new Commandant, but the explorer refuses; in fact, he tells the officer that he will do all in his power to put an end to the use of the death machine in the penal colony.

After a moment of disbelief, the officer frees the condemned man from the machine, telling him that his sentence has been repealed. The officer shows the explorer a new sentence—"Be Just"—and begins to realign the machine's mechanisms in order to write this. Finishing his work, the officer strips off his uniform, breaks his sword into pieces, and tosses all of his gear into a waste pit by the machine. Understanding what is about to happen but standing passively—almost approvingly—by, the explorer watches as the officer fits himself into the machine, which seems almost alive as it begins to work all by itself.

For a while the machine works perfectly and silently, but then all at once something begins to go wrong. Part of the machine opens and numerous gears begin to spill out. Completely breaking down, the machine fails to slowly write the death sentence on the officer's body: instead, it merely punctures him hundreds of times, killing him in just a few minutes instead of the "exquisite" twelve hours. When the explorer looks into the officer's face, he sees no sign of the "sixth hour" enlightenment that supposedly came upon the faces of the dying when the machine worked as it should. In a short finale to the tale, the explorer visits the grave of the old Commandant—it is located under a table in the colony's teahouse—then rather hastily leaves the island. The condemned man and the soldier who had been guarding him try to leave on the same boat as the explorer, but at the very end he waves them off, brandishing a large knotted rope to keep them at bay.

LIST OF CHARACTERS IN

"In the Penal Colony"

The main character of the story, **the explorer** acts as both witness and judge in the tale. Neither a member of the penal colony nor of its mother nation, the explorer is suspended between action and inertia. Fundamentally a moral man, he is repulsed and sickened by the officer, the machine, and what passes for justice in the penal colony; but at the same time, he holds himself in check because he respects the officer's dedication and obsession if not his actual deeds and beliefs. As a witness, he feels it is his duty to merely observe, but as the story progresses, the explorer learns that to witness is no mere passive act: to observe is to report, and to report is to judge. It is perhaps this "education" that helps to explain the identity the explorer feels with the officer at the end of the tale: since the enlightenment of the "sixth hour" has been denied to the officer, it is the enlightenment of the explorer that finally causes him to flee from the penal colony itself.

The officer is a man who has reached the end of his career—a career which has only existed because of the executions he has been in charge of. Alone in the colony because of his dedication to the old Commandant and because of his dedication to the death machine, the officer is obsessed with preserving existing traditions. Unable to see or understand anything that might challenge his role and sense of duty, the officer is at once blind and driven. For the officer, everything comes to have meaning only insofar as it relates to the machine; or put a better way, as far as the officer is concerned, the machine inscribes its meaning on everything. Justice itself comes to be identical with the machine, and so the officer gives himself up to it, having already come to understand that both his own time and that of the machine have passed.

CRITICAL VIEWS ON

"In the Penal Colony"

MALYNNE STERNSTEIN ON KAFKA'S USE OF HUMOR AGAINST INTERPRETATION

> [Malynne Sternstein is an assistant professor of Slavic literature and Germanic studies at the University of Chicago. She has also written *Against Arbitrariness. The Czech Avant-garde and the Subversion of the Symbolic Sign* and *Toyen: Gender, Obscurity and the Fires of Surrealism*. In this essay she contends that by focusing on the irony inherent in the story we are better able to see how Kafka understood the problem of both interpretation and of knowledge itself.]

Benjamin's reading of "In the Penal Colony" and its body in pain are informed by a modernist mission and he places more emphasis on guilt (interiority) than on shame (exteriority). The exquisite wounds carved on the soldier become a battleground between "those in power" and those subservient to it. The inscription in the flesh is a portal to the discovery of one's own (perhaps universal) guilt:

> an archaic apparatus . . . engraves ornate letters on the backs of guilty men, multiplying the cuts and increasing the ornamentation to the point where the back of the guilty man becomes clairvoyant, able itself to discover the writing from whose letters it must learn the name of its unknown guilt. It is, then, the back upon which this is incumbent."

Yet an alternate reading can employ the same descriptors to a variant conclusion. If the project of those in power is to fix the language of the Law onto the body of its citizens, to make it legible, Kafka's is to force this eminent "legibility" into "overexposure," which then "blocks every essay of interpretation." The struggle for signification—the officer's and the reader's—is laughable. What better language to defy paradigmatic signification than that of bodily praxis? This code of gesture, of bodily signs and postures, is Kafka's foremost language. It is one Benjamin not only noticed, praised, and analysed, but also criticized for its sometimes pathetic essentialism in his 1934 essay on the significance of the Kafkan gesture. For him, the allegory of Kafka's tales cannot be apprehended through the conventional complex of symbolic correspondences: Kafka's artistic force and vision lie within the "codex of gestures" and it is from here any understanding of his work must begin. The codex of gestures is one necessarily located in the body; no surprise then that Kafka is so concerned with the body's material potential for pain, wounding, breakage, and amputation. Pain, wounding, and decampment of the body are natural, if extreme, issues of a desire to restore the body to memory—to re-member the body—that recalls Benjamin's phrase, "the most forgotten alien land is one's own body." Benjamin senses a failure unspectacular in Kafka's gestural lexicon:

> In the mirror which the prehistoric world held before him in the form of guilt [Kafka] saw the future emerging in the form of a judgment. But he did not say what it was like. Kafka could understand things *only* in the form of a gestus, but he could not understand this *gestus* itself. In Kafka, narrative thus regains the significance it had in the mouth of Scheherazade: to postpone the future.

But this failure to unravel the full meaning of the *gestus* is the crucial moment of his postmodernity and as such the "procedure seems to us much more subversive than the usual modernist one, because the latter, by not showing the Thing, leaves open the possibility of grasping [its] central emptiness"—a process much more terrifying and liberating, and perhaps joyful, than the exposure of lack alone (*LA* 144–5). For Deleuze and Guattari, Kafka is less interested in "presenting the image of an unknowable law" than in "dissecting the mechanism" of the machines that use the idea of Law to set themselves in motion. "Because it has no object of knowledge," the machine is not the Law; "the law is operative only in being stated and stated only in the act of punishment: a statement directly inscribed on the real, on the body and the flesh." The punishment inscribed on the victim's flesh is a practical application of the Law, a shaming. Transcendence, proscribed or anticipated, has less to do with the sacrosanct character of the Law than with its vacuous need to be made meaningful by such gestures.

—Malynne Sternstein, "Laughter, Gesture, and Flesh: Kafka's 'In the Penal Colony'." *Modernism/Modernity* 8 (2001): pp. 315-23.

MARK ANDERSON ON THE BODY AS ART

> [Also the editor of *Reading Kafka: Prague, Politics, and the fin de siecle*, Mark Anderson is an Associate Professor of German and Comparative Literature at Columbia University. The following extract is drawn from *Kafka's Clothes: Ornament and Aestheticism in the Habsburg Fin* de Siecle, and explores ways in which Kafka's story represents how he considered himself a writer who has turned his own body and life into art.]

From this historical perspective we can now begin to read 'In the Penal Colony' not as a legal meditation on guilt and punishment, but as an ironic, self-reflexive commentary on Kafka's own literary production and its relation to contemporary aesthetic questions. First, one should note that the execution machine *writes* its judgement (the verb *schreiben* is repeated throughout the text), and that the product of its movements is consistently referred to as a text or as 'scripture' (*Schrift*). This writing is an artistic process, as numerous plays on the word for art indicate: the machine inscribes the judgement and embellishments into the prisoner's skin 'like a harrow' working the soul, but 'much more artfully' (*viel kunstgemässer*). Similarly, the master plan drawn by the former Commandant which guides the machine's writing of the arabesques is 'illegible' but 'sehr kunstvoll', literally 'full of art', a nuance obscured by the English translation of 'ingenious':

> [The officer] spread out the first sheet of paper. The explorer would have liked to say something appreciative, but all he could see was a labyrinth of lines crossing and recrossing each other, which covered the paper so thickly that it was difficult to discern the blank spaces between them. 'Read it', said the officer. 'I can't', said the explorer. 'Yet it's clear enough', said the officer. 'It's very artful', said the explorer evasively, 'but I can't make it out'. 'Yes', said the officer with a laugh, putting the paper away again, 'it's no calligraphy for school children.' (*CS* 148–9)

Often interpreted as the 'illegible' Hebrew characters of the Old Testament, these labyrinthine lines correspond to the embellishments which the machine, translating from the drawings, will inscribe as tattoos into the condemned man's body. Like the tattoo embellishments, these lines also evoke the swirling arabesques of *Jugendstil* ornament and by implication, Kafka's own *Jugendstil* writings. 'Artful' and abstract, they will transform the prisoner's body into a *Jugendstil* 'text', embellished with the appropriate marginalia.

This reading allows us to situate 'In the Penal Colony' not on a tropical island but on an 'island of tropes' (the German term 'Tropen' means both), a hermetic space for the fashioning of linguistic 'turns' of phrase. In German literature at the end of the nineteenth century, the island was a common figure for the autonomy of art. In innumerable writings by Stefan George, Heinrich Mann, Hermann Hesse, and Rilke, it served as a convenient shorthand for the *Insel der Kunst*, or art-for-art's-sake movement. Hesse's novella 'Inseltraum' ('Island Dream', 1899), is typical in this respect and gave the *Jugendstil* movement, as Jürg Mathes observes, 'one of its most significant catchwords.' The same image was adopted by the Insel publishing house as an emblem for the autonomous, hermetic work of literary art.

> —Mark Anderson, "The Ornaments of Writing: 'In the Penal Colony'." *Kafka's Clothes: Ornament and Aestheticism in the Habsburg* Fin de Siecle, (Oxford: Clarendon Press, 1992): pp. 173-193.

Arnold Weinstein on the Impossibility of a Final Interpretation for the Story

> [Arnold Weinstein is the Edna and Richard Salomon Distinguished Professor and Professor of Comparative Literature, English and French Studies at Brown University. He has also written *The Fiction of Relationship and Fictions of the Self, 1550-1800.* Here, he argues against the interpretation of Kafka's story; in its stead he contends that Kafka's purpose in the tale is to focus on the processes of communication and on language itself.]

Many find "In the Penal Colony" a grisly, brutal story. Like the story of the exodus from the Garden, it is about the cost of knowledge. We are so accustomed to defining knowledge as information, so habituated to language as explanatory, that the high stakes and cruel outcomes of Kafka's parable seem melodramatic or Gothic. But his story depicts, with rare power, the drama of human understanding. In Borges' fine essay, "Kafka and his Precursors," he suggests that great art creates new constellations, that we see, as critics, both backwards and forwards in our efforts to discern intellectual kinship between authors. Kafka's metamorphic view of relationship and knowledge may serve as a model for literature's claim to tell us about Others. Using Borges as precedent, I would like to suggest two particular texts which leave us with the same dark knowledge. Melville's tortured tale, "Benito Cereno," depends entirely on point-of-view narrative, thereby showing that the perfectly innocent mind cannot see evil. But the underside of Melville's story is the unwritten narrative, the experience of Cereno himself which the reader begins to understand only when the tale is over. Masquerading as a white man in control, Cereno has in fact been forced to obey his Black "slaves" at every turn; the reader has seen the innocent version of events, but Cereno has experienced *from the inside*, the collapse of his role, the reality of the Blacks. And he dies. In somewhat similar manner, Faulkner's *Absalom, Absalom!* dramatizes the cost of knowledge: in this case, the two college boys, Quentin and Shreve, must somehow go beyond the data of history if they are to understand the past; in extremely elaborate ways, they achieve what Faulkner calls an "overpass to love," as they "become" the protagonists of the Civil War and experience, again from the inside, the human feelings that make up history, in this case, a bloody history of fratricide, both personal and national. Yet, here too, Faulkner does not minimize the cost of such an "overpass," and the book closes on a note of futility and exhaustion, a keen sense that we can become the Other only momentarily, and even then at the cost of our own integrity. The Melville and Faulkner examples are not properly metamorphic, but they have the same cardinal truth at their heart: knowledge of the other entails eclipse of the self, and can lead to death as well as to love.

Beyond even the metamorphosis, however, there is the machine. Kafka's writing machine is a mad figure for the role of art and understanding in a world filled exclusively with signs and flesh. How can signs and flesh be connected, the thickness of matter be penetrated by the logos of spirit? The Word of the past, the Word that spoke Truth and commanded Assent, is gone. But the writer remains. Kafka's machine depicts the need that every writer has felt for a language so potent, that it would become the reality whereof it speaks. The writing machine bespeaks and, *à sa façon*, remedies the absence of understanding in a degraded world: the animal body has no access to its soul; the individuals attain no contact with each other. The machine is indeed intolerable in its flagrant violation of the body, but it functions as a sublime symbol of Kafka's—and all artists'—aspirations: to read his work is to be penetrated by it; his words are inscribed in our flesh; our understanding of the story, of the Other, is to be both visceral and transcendent. The text is the machine: the metamorphosis is in us.

—Arnold Weinstein, "Kafka's Writing Machine: Metamorphosis in the Penal Colony." *Critical Essays on Franz Kafka*, by Ruth V. Gross, (Boston: G.K. Hall & Co.: 1990): pp. 120-129.

ALLEN THIHER ON WRITING AS ACCESS TO THE LAW

[This extract taken form *Franz Kafka: A Study of the Short Fiction* tries to show how Kafka's punning approach in the story shows that writing and the Law are two sides of the same operation.]

"In the Penal Colony" spells out, as pun and literally, that the law and writing are two sides of the same thing—of that unnameable logos that we assume must exist. Writing is, in a quite literal sense, the means of finding access to the law, and hence to redemption, justification, and salvation. (Erlösung is the received term for salvation that Kafka uses, derisively, in the story itself.) In this exemplary story, then, the equation between writing and the law is savagely clear: writing is a way of finding the law as well as the force of the law itself.

The identification of writing with the law is given literal expression by the story's writing and punishing machine. This machine is far more than a simple torture device that seems to foreshadow our science fiction dreams of what one might achieve with the proper application of cybernetics. It is a machine that writes the law, or if one prefers, inscribes revelation in the flesh. In the story's bizarre prison colony there is no need for trials, or even for the condemned to be told their crime, because the writing machine grants the condemned a revelation of the law when it writes the law on the body of the prisoner who is strapped in the machine. By granting access to the law through this inscription, by making the word flesh as it were, the machine should bring about the promised redemption that the story's protagonist, the explorer, looks for, but does not find when the machine's guardian immolates himself on it.

—Allen Thiher, "'In the Penal Colony'," *Franz Kafka: A Study of the Short Fiction*, (Boston: Twayne: 1990): pp. 51-67.

Clayton Koelb on the Reading Process

[Clayton Koelb is a professor of Germanic Languages and Literature at the University of Chicago. He is also the author of *The Incredulous Reader: Literature and the Effects of Disbelief* and *Inventions of Reading: Rhetoric and the Literary Imagination*. In this selection from *Kafka's Rhetoric*, Koelb argues that too much emphasis has been placed on "writing" in interpreting the story, and that the story can be better interpreted as an examination of Kafka's theory of reading.]

In the theory of reading implicit here, the reader does not act upon the text, but rather the text takes the initiative and acts upon the reader. The reader submits, and this submission is all the reader needs to do. The book then takes charge and both picks up the reader and forces its way inside him. The text writes upon the reader and even makes him into a kind of copy of itself.

Kafka's scene of writing, then, is really just as much a scene of reading. There is, in fact, little distinction to be made between writing and reading in this mythology, wherein reading is understood to be the passive reception of an aggressive and powerful text. Writing is the creation of a template that directs an act of inscription, and reading is the suffering of that inscription upon the reader's psyche. Obviously, what is needed is a mechanism to mediate, to bring the writer's template text into contact with the reader's psychic matrix. Kafka's machine has just this function. It does not *record* the words of the Old Commandant; rather it makes those words, previously recorded on paper, sensible to the condemned prisoner. The officer possesses the holograph manuscript of what represents to him the most sacred scripture: "'I am still using the guiding plans drawn by the former Commandant. Here they are'—he extracted some sheets from the leather wallet—'but I'm sorry I can't let you handle them, they are my most precious possessions.'" The task of the machine is not simply to write the commandments of paternal authority—the Old Commandant has in fact already written them, all of them, and given them to the officer—but to make that writing legible to the victim. Kafka is careful to make clear that, as marks on paper, the writing of the Old Commandant is not legible at all: "The explorer would have liked to say something appreciative, but all he could see was a labyrinth of lines crossing and recrossing each other, which covered the paper so thickly that it was difficult to discern the blank spaces between them. 'Read it,' said the officer. 'I can't,' said the explorer. 'Yet it's clear enough,' said the officer." This scripture, then, already exists in the documents preserved by the officer. It has already been written. The function of the machine is to make the scripture comprehensible to the prisoner. In other words, its chief job is to serve as the means by which one may read what is written. And this reading takes time. "Man muß lange darin lesen." The machine ensures that the condemned man will spend an average of twelve hours in continuous study, at the end of which time he will be dead.

—Clayton Koelb, *Kafka's Rhetoric: The Passion of Reading* (Ithica, Cornell University Press, 1989): pp. 74–75.

PLOT SUMMARY OF

"A Hunger Artist"

"A Hunger Artist" tells the story of an obsessed man whose profession and art is fasting. In the old days, the hunger artist was a figure of awe and respect for the populace, and staging one of his fasting performances was profitable for him and his partner. People would visit the cage in which he spent the fast every day to watch him as he sat on a bed of straw, sometimes responding to questions from the crowd, occasionally holding out a thin arm to show how bony he'd become, but most often as he simply sat there withdrawn into the innermost part of himself.

We learn that the hunger artist takes his fasting as just that—an art—and he is fervently devoted to his craft. Children find him especially inspiring, even if their elders often scoff at the artist and claim he is somehow swindling them all, but the artist himself takes the most interest in those who are hired by the impresario to watch him and make sure that the fast is legitimate. Many of the professional watchers, thinking they are helping him, withdraw from the cage at night, presumably to give him the chance to eat some food he has carefully hidden in the straw or on his person. But far from pleasing him, these watchers enrage him, both because they assume he is cheating in his art and because nothing he can do or say convinces them that he is a hard and honest worker. He much prefers the skeptical watchers who never leave the side of the cage, who are always on guard to catch him in his tricks. These he respects, and he takes pleasure in proving to them that he is truly fasting.

But even the careless, unbelieving watchers are not what upsets him the most. In fact, he is his own greatest disappointment. Not only is he alone in understanding what fasting actually means—and how easy it actually is—but, he finds that he wishes he could continue his fasting past the proscribed limit.

Because of the public's attention span—it remains keenly interested in the fast for only so long—by tradition the fasting period lasts "only" forty days. At the end of that time, a great ceremony is held, and the artist is led from his cage (dragged in fact) and forced to eat a bit of food. Among speeches, general fanfare, and rousing music, the end of the fast is announced, and all are satisfied in the end—all that is, except for the hunger artist, who wishes to extend his fasting indefinitely.

For many years the hunger artist and the impresario enjoy great fame and attention, all at once, though perhaps not without warning, the public's taste for fasting wanes, and the hunger artist finds himself less and less often at the center of attention. When at last it seems as if the revulsion against fasting and the hunger artist have become nearly universal, he leaves his partner and takes up with a large circus, hoping to find peace and quiet and perhaps a little attention—much to his chagrin, he finds neither.

His own cage is placed near the circus' animal cages, and while throngs pass by him, few, if any, take notice of him let alone have any understanding of what he is doing. His cage, at first brightly decorated with placards and a tally of his days fasted, eventually falls into a shabby state of disrepair. Eventually, even the circus staff takes little notice of him and finally forgets about him altogether. Not at all alarmed by this development, the hunger artist continues his fast, unnoticed and unrecognized, but still hoping to break all past records for fasting.

Eventually, an overseer with the circus spots the apparently empty cage and wonders what a perfectly useful piece of equipment is doing there unused. No one can remember why the cage is even there, but finally someone recalls something about a hunger artist. They begin to poke about in the straw, and ultimately they find the emaciated artist is indeed still there, still fasting.

When asked when he intends to stop fasting, the hunger artist asks for their forgiveness rather than offering an answer. He tells the circus workers that all he ever wanted was to be admired, and when they go along with him and say that they do admire him, he answers that they shouldn't. Thinking him fully out of his mind, the overseer asks why his fasting shouldn't be admired. The hunger artist tells him that his fasting is unworthy of admiration because he can't help but fast. And why can't he help it? Because, the hunger artist answers, he could never find the food he liked. If he had been able to, he assures them, he wouldn't have eaten his fill, the same as they. With these words, the hunger artist dies. And with no further ado, the overseer immediately has him buried along with the filthy straw that had lined his cage. The cage itself is cleaned and in it is placed a healthy young panther. At the end of the story, people crowd around the panther's cage, both shocked by and drawn to the power and freedom the animal exudes.

LIST OF CHARACTERS IN

"A Hunger Artist"

The Hunger Artist, the only true character in the tale, is a man driven by an obsession to fast longer than anyone else ever has. A true artist, he demands perfection of himself, and at the same time is continually disappointed by what he knows are his shortcomings. Both dependent on and repelled by the response and understanding of the public, he is constantly suspended between uncertainty and disgust. Unable to accept the change in public taste, he goes on fasting with essentially no recognition, purely because he seeks to outdo the record for fasting: a record he himself has obviously set. Thus, while his motivation is unclear—until the very end of the story at least—he is essentially trying to outpace himself, trying to best himself as best he can as it were.

CRITICAL VIEWS ON

"A Hunger Artist"

KURT FICKERT ON THE UNRELIABLE NARRATOR IN THE STORY

[Kurt Fickert is Professor Emeritus of German at Wittenberg University. He is the author of *End of a Mission: Kafka's Search for Truth in His Last Stories* as well as many articles on Kafka and Czech and German literature. In this selection from *End of a Mission*, Fickert argues that the unreliability of the narrator in the story does not, as some critics have suggested, lend a humorous tone to the story but rather further develops Kafka's theme of the tragic role of the artist in society.]

The crucial function that the presence of an unreliable narrator would have to have, in my understanding, would be to serve as a double for the impresario. The latter is, as the fact that he is not named, but only designated by his occupation attests, the intermediary between the hunger artist and the public. At an important turning point in the performer's career, he dismisses his booking agent and manager; when he disappears from the scene, it seems clear that Kafka has allowed the "personalized" narrator to take over his role. The essential part he plays in the story consists of his bringing it to a close, for he reports events which occur after the hunger artist's death, including the climactic one of the replacement of the exhibit of the fasting man by the exhibit of the ravenous panther. The doubling which occurs in "Ein Hungerkünstler" is not without precedent in the Kafka canon; K's two assistants in *Das Schloß*, the two celluloid balls in "Blumfeld, ein älterer Junggeselle" ("Blumfeld, an Elderly Bachelor"), and, to a considerable extent, Robinson and Delamarch in *Amerika* are prominent examples of the use of this device in Kafka's fiction. Both the impresario and the narrator show sympathy for the person who apparently has been impelled to perform a strange and difficult task in the public arena, but they understand neither the significance of his act nor the nature of the torment he inflicts on himself. In this regard the two represent the members of the society, the common lot of people, within which and in relation to which the artist makes his presentation. For the public, art which claims to have a higher purpose than that of entertaining an audience or of diverting their attention away very briefly from their quotidian cares and responsibilities lies in an extraneous area of their lives. (Obviously, the impresario whose livelihood is earned by providing entertainment for the masses has for this reason more concern for the artist's tribulations than they do.)

—Kurt Fickert, *End of a Mission: Kafka's Search for Truth in His Last Stories*. Columbia, SC: Camden House (1993).

FRANK VULPI ON THE FAUSTIAN ASPECTS OF THE STORY

[Frank Vulpi is a professor in the dance department at the University of North Carolina. Here he argues that 'The Hunger Artist' is a representation of the "Faustian man": a remorseless contender after something extraordinary.]

If an individual pursues an idea or creates something primarily to please himself, gain power, or satisfy his ego, then the originator of that idea or creation can properly be termed a Faustian man.

Does Kafka call into question the wisdom of the Faustian man? I think he does. Kafka's hunger artist is a powerful example of a Faustian man who, in his preoccupation with his ego and personal objectives has become irrevocably estranged from his community and the life around him.

The alternative to working primarily for oneself and towards goals which are established by the individual (and consequently often valuable or relevant only to that individual) is to work in community with others towards a common goal. (. . .)

The hunger artist is a most extreme illustration of the Faustian man: as he reaches perfection in his work (that is, as he starves himself longer and longer) he naturally approaches death and thus, not only figuratively, but literally dies to the possibility of communion.

—Frank Vulpi, "Kafka's 'A Hunger Artist': A Cautionary Tale for Faustian Man Caught Between Creativity and Communion." *Germanic Notes and Reviews* 24 (1993): pp. 9-12.

Breon Mitchell on the Factual Precedents for Kafka's Story

[Breon Mitchell is a professor of contemporary literature and Germanic studies at Indiana University. He has translated Martin Grzimek's *Heartstop* and is the editor of Ezra Pound's own translations of Paul Morand's *Fancy Goods/Open All Night*. In this essay, Mitchell points out that far from fable or allegory, Kafka's story has an historical, factual precedent: there were real hunger artists in Kafka's time.]

Many of the general characteristics of Kafka's hunger artist were shared by more than one professional faster and might have been known to Kafka from any of several sources. Given the inevitable boredom of confinement during a long fast, for example, it is not surprising that stories were often told to pass the time. Tanner was reported to have spent most of his days lying in bed, reading newspapers, or "in conversation with his watchers." Succi's tales had even included affairs of the heart: "he told the young men serving as watchers during the fast about an amorous adventure during his thirty day fast in Paris." And even on the thirty-first day of his fast, A. Levanzin, the subject chosen for the Carnegie Institution's experiment, "talked very rapidly and in a lively manner for nearly 40 minutes." Kafka's hunger artist talks in order to show those watching him that he is not eating: "he was ready to exchange jokes with them, to tell them stories out of his nomadic life, anything at all to keep them awake and demonstrate to them again that he had no eatables in his cage and that he was fasting as not one of them could fast."

Succi's sense of honor and pride was also shared by at least a few other hunger artists. Levanzin, who set out explicitly to break Succi's thirty day record (which had remained the longest scientifically controlled fast), impressed the members of Carnegie's research team by his integrity: "Throughout the fast he was under constant surveillance by various responsible members of the staff and there were nearly always two or three assistants on duty in the room. It was therefore impossible for him to leave the balcony or to obtain food without its being known at once. . . . Moreover, he had too much interest in the fast to do anything of the kind, and we firmly believe that if he had been surreptitiously offered food, he would have, refused it." The resemblance of this passage to the parallel situation in Kafka's text is remarkable: "there were also relays of permanent watchers . . . and it was their task to watch the hunger artist day and night, three of them at a time, in case he should have some secret recourse to nourishment. This was nothing but a formality . . . for the initiates knew well enough that during his fast the artist would never in any circumstances, not even under forcible compulsion, swallow the smallest morsel of food; the honor of his profession forbade it."

Like Kafka's hunger artist, Levanzin was noticeably depressed by the fact that he was not allowed to fast for a longer period of time. Toward the end of his fast he became irritable and "complained bitterly to Dr. Langfeld regarding Mr. Carpenter [one of the staff], saying that he would like to break every bone in his body," which, as the author dryly noted, "would pronounce against fasting for amiability." Levanzin told Dr. Langfeld "that he was very sorry that [they] wanted him to break the fast and that he could easily fast for 10 days more," and "when seen five months after the fast was broken, he appeared rather unhappy. . . . He was plainly disappointed because the world had not given him the recognition due him for the sacrifice he had made for the benefit of mankind." As the narrator of "A Hunger Artist" says, "he was working honestly, but the world was cheating him of his reward."

But Kafka knew more about hunger artists than just their temperaments and their code of honor. He was also clearly familiar with the main facets of fasting as a form of public entertainment. Except in the unlikely event that he had actually witnessed such a display, he must have learned about them through newspaper reports, for even in "the great cities" these spectacles were covered on a daily basis by the press. Some hunger artists simply conducted their fasts under observation while living in lodgings, and felt free to take walks in the park, or go for carriage rides around the city. Others, however, were under stricter management, and were presented by their impresarios in the amphitheatres of one or the other of the great public exhibition halls such as the Crystal Palace and the Royal

Aquarium in London, or the Panoptikum in Berlin. Spectators were charged admission, although of course there was little to see. Reports indicate, however, that visitors streamed in and were allowed to talk to and question the hunger artists. These were exhibitions "under one's own management," as Kafka puts it, financially independent of any other acts or performances.

—Breon Mitchell, "Kafka and 'The Hunger Artist'." *Kafka and the Contemporary Critical Performance*, ed. Alan Udoff, (Bloomington: Indiana University Press, 1987): pp. 236-255.

Nathan Cervo on the Satirical Nature of the Story

[Nathan Cervo was a poet and professor of English at Franklin Pierce College. In this essay, Cervo asserts that the story is a combination of a shaggy dog story and a Jewish joke that parodies both the Nativity and the Epiphany.]

The chief character in Franz Kafka's short story "A Hunger Artist" (1924) has one talent, which he professionalizes, that of starving himself. Eventually, due to lack of popular interest, he is relegated to a side cage, where he languishes on straw, almost indistinguishable from it—a parody of both the Nativity and the Epiphany.

On one level, Kafka is telling both a shaggy-dog story and a Jewish joke. When the chief character, really dying from starvation this time, has a chance to deliver the punch line, he does: he has fasted, he confesses to the overseer, because he couldn't find any food he liked. In the style of the Jewish joke, he deflates all speculations involving the overblown or pretentious.

After a career that featured listlessness, abulia, and obsession, during which he starves himself rigorously and apparently gratuitously (therefore "artistically"), the hunger artist's appeal begins to wane. In an effort to regain popularity, he starves himself to death. Then the foul straw in his cage is swept out, and a new attraction is installed to delight the crowd: a panther—sinuous, voluptuous, young, and vital. The etymons of the word "panther" (Greek *pan* and *ther*: "all," "beast") suggest the Dionysian, or Bacchic, aura emanated by the story's subtext. In ancient depictions, the Theban Bacchus carries a thyrsus, and a panther generally lies at his feet.

In Kafka's parable, it is Jesus who signifies the divine intoxication, the vital "freedom," bestowed by the Christian mysteries: Christianity surcharges its undaunted believers with the authentic gusto that is the existentially kept promise of faith, hope, and charity.

Kafka was a sophisticated Czech Jew and must have been aware of certain bizarre accounts of Jesus' genealogy. (For data and epithets pertaining to these accounts, see Strack and Billerbeck, *Kommentar zum Neuen Testament aus Talmud und Midrasch*, 4 vols., Munich, 1922–28, particularly 1, 33ff, 42–43, 1040, and 4. 1240.) According to these often self-contradictory accounts, Jesus the Nosri (Nazarene) was born of a hairdresser named Mary. The true father of Jesus was a certain *Panthera*, sometimes identified as a Roman soldier. Assuming good faith on the part of some of these chroniclers, the name *Panthera* might have resulted from a mishearing of the Greek genitive form of *parthenos* ("unmarried woman"). The phrase *huios parthenou* ("son of an unmarried woman") might have been misheard as huios pantherou ("son of Panthera"). Jesus is frequently called a "bastard" in these accounts.

In light of the above, and given Kafka's yearning treatment of Catholicism in his novel *Der Prozess* (*The Trial*, 1925), it is easy to see why the free and joyful presence of a panther is necessary to Kafka's fulfilled meaning in "A Hunger Artist." The panther (Jesus) may be caged (systematized) but "freedom" is seen by "even the most insensitive" "to lurk" "in his jaws" (tr. Edwin and Willa Muir, 1948). Calumny is thus transformed ironically to soothsaying, and here, in this symbol of the panther, is the New Dispensation.

Which shall it be—the Endura, the fast unto death of the old Jewish mystics, or the panther's revelry?

—Nathan Cervo, "Kafka's 'A Hunger Artist'." *Explicator* 50 (1992): p. 99-100.

Joseph M. Garrison on the Collective Power of Art

[Joseph M. Garrison is a professor emeritus of English at Mary Baldwin College. He has written extensively on Poe, Kafka, and others. In this essay, he contends that the story is not so much about the alienation of the artist from society but rather it is about the ways in which art affects society deeply enough to bring all of its members together.]

The narrator styles himself, for example, as an observer of "professional fasting" (p. 268); he describes the events as "thrilling performances" (p. 275) in which "the whole effect was heightened by torch flares" (p. 268); he speaks of "records" (p. 276), "rewards" (p. 276), the "art of fasting" (p. 276), and " placards" (p. 276); he details, almost too fastidiously, the responsibilities and maneuverings of "the impresario" (p. 272). If the narrator is detached, his "detachment" creates a very curious and problematical pattern. Out of context, his dilettantism could be construed as a pose, taken for the purpose of critique. The whole story, however, indicates that the narrator genuinely subscribes to this value system and considers himself one of the few "initiates" (p. 270) who can genuinely appreciate the hunger artist. Item: every group of people in the story is held up to scorn, ridicule, or sarcasm for their failure to be knowledgeable in the art of fasting or for their willingness to abandon themselves to impulse once the task of "watching" is over. No one except the narrator and the artist, it seems, is capable of understanding; for others, enlightenment is "quite impossible" (p. 268). Hence, the narrator refers to the need of "the masses" (p. 268) to be reassured; and he observes that "not every watcher, of course, was capable of understanding" (p. 269) why the artist "would never in any circumstances, not even under forcible compulsion, swallow the smallest morsel of food." (pp. 268–269) He is openly contemptuous of the "people who argued that this breakfast was an unfair attempt to bribe the watchers" (p. 269) and preens himself, at the expense of others, by mentioning conditions "hardly to be understood by well-fed people" (p. 272). The artist's misery, the narrator thinks, is caused by the public's insensitivity: "So he lived for many years, with small regular intervals of recuperation, in visible glory, honored by the world, yet in spite of that troubled in spirit, and all the more troubled because no one would take his trouble seriously" (p. 272).

But does *the narrator* actually take the artist "seriously"? Or is he the most extreme example in the story of a lack of seriousness? The latter alternative seems more tenable, particularly in view of the cognitive priorities that are revealed in the narrator's language. In almost every paragraph, we have evidence of a purely visual orientation and a purely visual perception of art; references to eyes and seeing almost become a signature. Additionally, we have the logic of "good reason" (p. 270) and the conclusions that "experience had proved" (p. 270), implying an analytical approach to reality and an attempt to explain art as if its essence could be grasped by recognizing the "premonitory symptoms" (p. 273) and finding the "profound causes" (p. 273). The narrator assumes that he, like the hunger artist, knows "the real situation" (p. 274); and at one point he actually flaunts his enlightened status: "To fight against this lack of understanding, against a whole world of nonunderstanding, was impossible" (p. 273). Or again, even more presumptuously: "Just try to explain to anyone the art of fasting! Anyone who has no feeling for it cannot be made to understand" (p. 276). And throughout the story, of course, there is a clear-cut differentiation between the "I" as connoisseur and the bumblings of the passersby with their "indifference and inborn malice" (p. 276).

Read in this way, Kafka's story is not an allegory with *cri de coeur* reverberations. It comes close, both in meaning and spirit, to Dylan Thomas's "In My Craft and Sullen Art." In that poem, Thomas tells us that he writes for the "common wages" of lovers. He does not write for proud men, nor for those who think his art is a commodity, nor for those who praise his craft or art, but for those who are experientially affected by what he has to say, who understand why he is "sullen" and who respond to the situation by taking the griefs of *the ages* into their arms and loving *them*, thereby spending the "common wages" not on a work of art for the art's sake but on the acts of love which Thomas's art commends. It seems to me that Kafka is saying essentially the same thing about the writer's concern for sufficient love among people and that he uses the narrator in "A Hunger Artist" to make essentially the same point he had made much earlier in his career in a letter to Oskar Pollack: "What we need are books that affect us like some really grievous misfortune, like the death of one whom we loved more than ourselves, as if we were banished to distant forests, away from everybody, like a suicide; a book must be the ax for the frozen sea within us. That is what I believe." Only readers can provide the food that would satisfy the hunger artist, and that food is found in a selfless commitment to the human agony of the world—a total immersion and not merely a spectatorial adventure.

—Joseph M. Garrison, "Getting into the Cage: A Note on Kafka's 'A Hunger Artist'." *International Fiction Review* 8 (1981): p. 61-63.

PLOT SUMMARY OF

"Josephine the Singer and the Mousefolk"

"Our singer is called Josephine. Anyone who has not heard her does not know the power of song": so begins the narrative of Kafka's tale of the mouse folk and the role that singing—and by implication, art in general—plays in their community. From the introductory sentences, we might expect to hear a litany of praises for Josephine and her voice as well as a grand description of song itself, but Kafka gives us something quite different in this puzzling tale.

The narrator tells us that the mouse folk are essentially unmusical, and that when Josephine eventually leaves them, music will also disappear from their lives. Given this lack of interest in music, how is it, the narrator wonders, that the mouse folk can understand Josephine and her art at all? The answer, as we might expect from Kafka, is that they don't understand it at all—something which Josephine herself firmly avows as well. It is actually at this point in the ongoing narration that Kafka actually begins the story. The narrator attempts to explain Josephine's singing so as to understand it as best he can, but what he finds more than anything else is that the concept of "understanding" is wholly inappropriate and inadequate when confronted by the enigma of Josephine and her singing. That is, "understanding" itself is not up to the task of interpreting Josephine or art.

The first tangible thing we learn is that far from having an exceptional voice, Josephine has at best an ordinary one. The narrator informs us that far from being exceptional, Josephine's singing is hardly singing at all: it is at most a piping—rather, not even an ordinary piping, but a weak and ill-sounding piping which even the simplest of the mouse folk can surpass. What then, the narrator wonders, is the real nature of the incredible effect Josephine has on the mouse folk?

From this first reversal of expectations, the narrator proceeds through a series of convoluted contradictions on his path to understanding: her piping is weak and even sub-ordinary, but her actual performances constitute magnificent ceremonies; Josephine actually has no real skill at all, but once in her presence, a listener becomes enlightened; it is impossible to distinguish between the singing of a well-rehearsed Josephine and the impromptu piping of a child interrupting Josephine's performance, yet such an interruption is immediately squelched by the mouse folk as a whole. And it is through this series of apparent contradictions that the narrator first glimpses the actual nature of Josephine's singing: he tells us that Josephine's singing is so influential not because it teaches understanding, but because it teaches "awed respect."

But the narrator refuses to let the matter stand there. He then begins to wonder why the mouse folk make so much effort to accommodate Josephine—who after all, is nothing more than a pampered diva at best, a spoiled child at worst. Are the mouse folk unconditionally devoted to Josephine? No, they are not capable of unconditional devotion to anyone or anything yet they are devoted to her nevertheless. Can they laugh at what is ridiculous in Josephine? No, that would be impossible—but there *is* so much in Josephine that is entirely laughable. Do the mouse folk, in times of trouble or danger, find solace or inspiration in Josephine? No, she and her singing offer neither salvation nor strength, yet in desperate emergencies, the mouse folk flock to Josephine even more than under normal conditions.

Spinning through another series of contradictions that Josephine's importance produces—for example, far from saving the mouse folk from danger, Josephine's singing, because it brings the mouse folk all together in one place, actually exposes them to more danger—the narrator at last has to confront a basic truth: neither Josephine's importance nor her own desires can be put into words.

At this point, just as the narrator comes up against the enigma that is art itself, he tells us that Josephine has disappeared from the community. Though perhaps this disappearance is simply a ruse, just another part of her campaign to be exempted from her normal chores and obligations as a worker, the narrator believes it is actually a severe miscalculation on Josephine's part. Instead of reacting adversely to her disappearance, and even though they are all looking for her, none of the mouse folk are affected by her absence, and they go on as if nothing has happened. At the end of the story, the narrator predicts that silence will overtake the mouse folk now that

Josephine is gone for good—but even this realization is undercut or contradicted by the narrator's realization that Josephine's singing was essentially already silent. The riddle of Josephine and her singing, we are told, is the riddle of silence itself, the labyrinth in which everything is eventually forgotten.

LIST OF CHARACTERS IN

"Josephine the Singer and the Mousefolk"

The singer **Josephine** is the only named character in the story, and really the only individualized character at all. A figure of intense—one might even say *infinite*—contradictions, it is almost impossible to describe her or to explain her motivations. As the narrator comes to realize, it is actually the indescribable nature of Josephine that comes closest to describing her—but in keeping with the story as a whole, this doesn't come at all close to describing her. Arrogant yet timid; lazy but conscientious; demanding yet pleasant; assertive yet passive; crafty yet naïve—all of these, as well as any number of other impossible characteristics, begin to delineate Josephine, to allow her to stand out as it were, while hardly doing justice to her or her art at all.

CRITICAL VIEWS ON

"Josephine the Singer and the Mousefolk"

LAURENCE A. RICKELS ON THE PHANTASMAL ASPECTS OF JOSEPHINE'S SINGING

[Laurence A. Rickels is a professor of German at the University of California, Santa Barbara. He is the author of *The Vampire Lectures, Aberrations of Mourning*, and *The Case of California*. Here, he suggests that Josephine's singing is best described as a kind of phantom: a silence that marks the missing or abbreviated childhood of the mouse-folk.]

But in "The Judgment" Kafka read loud and clear that a father's authority consists of tapping into and usurping a son's rapport with phantoms: according to the father, the phantom friend in Russia both does not exist and writes only and ultimately to the father. What remains is the father's superegoical command from which the son cannot swerve since he carries inside his illegitimate cargo which the superego, as Freud makes clear in *The Ego and the Id*, is programmed to abort. Thus the condition of the pact or game with the encrypted brothers—that both parties either stay or go—is transformed into terms of a suicide pact: the melancholic son, at the close of "The Judgment," fulfills the terms of the contract which, according to the father, he put out on himself.

In his diary entry of September 25, 1917, Kafka wrote: "I could thus entrust myself to death. Vestige of a belief. Return to father. Great day of reconciliation." By its transformation into a return to father, the Russian mission opened onto the suicide mission it had only contained. At the end of the double mission which "The Judgment" first projected outward and which the mice in 1917 returned close-range, Kafka conceived, inside his father's house, the testament of two stories. "The Burrow" returns by amplifying the noise of mice devouring from within the walls around and in Kafka. In "Josephine the Singer or the Mousefolk," the rodent's solo panic finds its diagnosis or prolongation within a culture industry which places a phantom at the center of group identifications harboring the father. Josephine's song is part children's piping, part silence; her spectacular disappearance—which was always already in place—doubles the absence of childhood in a culture where all, accordingly, remain childish. The babbling child to whom the "paternal group" turns a "deaf ear" is missing—neither living nor dead—while, in her missingness, she remains a primal object of identification within mass culture.

—Laurence A. Rickels, "MUSICPHANTOMS: 'Uncanned' Conceptions of Music from Josephine the Singer to Mickey Mouse." *SubStance: A Review of Theory and Literary Criticism* 18 (1989): p. 3-24.

Ruth V. Gross on the Importance of Josephine's Female Voice

[Ruth V. Gross is a professor of German at the University of Texas, Arlington. She is the editor of *Critical Essays on Franz Kafka* and the author of *PLAN and the Austrian Rebirth: Portrait of a Journal*. In this essay, Gross suggests that it is specifically Josephine's feminine voice that is the center of and central to the story.]

Josefine—the name defines her being, her essence. It is the feminine form of Joseph, Kafka's protagonist in "The Trial." In other words, it is Joseph with an appendage, a tail, if you will—a something extra that makes her feminine. Although the something extra usually defines the male, with mice it is different. The appendage-tail turns her from a man named Joseph into a female mouse. Of course, Joseph was also a patriarch of the Hebrews. As Moses led the Exodus out, Joseph led the Eisodus in before him. If, as Brod and other critics have suggested, the mousepeople are the people of Moses, the "ine," the supplement, the tail, could be seen as being caught between the two biblical patriarchs Joseph and Moses. The title, as Kafka finally revised it—"Josefine die Sängerin oder das Volk der Mäuse"—reflects this. It is this name—Josefine—that lets the readers know that the singer of note here is female. The text portrays the mousepeople as a patriarchal society. Their attitude toward Josefine is paternal. In this society she, most of all, is the different one. She stands out, not only by virtue of her name, but because of her actions. As they patronize her, protect her, keep her in line, i.e., father her, she believes that by bringing them together, she protects them, saves them, gives them strength, dominates them, i.e., mothers them. The name becomes the semantic indicator of difference—that which makes Josefine Josefine—the other, the mother of her people.

—Ruth V. Gross, "Of Mice and Women: Reflections on a Discourse in Kafka's 'Josefine, die Sangerin oder Das Volk der Mause'." *The Germanic Review* 60 (1985): pp. 59-68.

J. P. Stern on the Redefinition of Kafka's Oeuvre

[J. P. Stern was a professor in the University College of London's Institute of Germanic Studies. He wrote *The Dear Purchase: A Theme in German Modernism, A Study of Nietzsche*, and edited *The World of Franz Kafka*. In this critical piece, Stern suggests that because the story doesn't fit with the rest of Kafka's tales in many way, that it redefines the "total" conception of Kafka's work.]

The story began as inconspicuously as possible, simply because it had to begin somehow; and it ends almost as inconspicuously, in ripples and echoes. For some reason that is never fully disclosed but which is connected with her failure to have her status recognized, her uniqueness accepted, Josephine has gone into hiding; at least, 'she has disappeared, she doesn't want to sing, she doesn't even want to be asked to sing, this time she has left us entirely' ('sie hat uns diesmal völlig verlassen'). Which is it to be: 'diesmal' or 'völlig'? Does she merely calculate on a triumphant return? She is the prima donna to the end. Has she miscalculated? Or has she spent herself, given her life for the power of her song? Did she really speak the truth when, pleading to be granted the privileges she felt were due to her art, she claimed she was the victim of exhaustion, of self-sacrifice? She has gone away. Died, perhaps? The tone of the story is gentle throughout, yet here, right at the end, Kafka is intent on giving it an added strength. One thinks of the words he himself used at the end of his life, when, afraid that his friends were leaving him alone, he called out to them to stay. 'I am not going away', one of his friends said. 'But I,' he said, and we read that he said it in a strong voice, 'But I am going away!"

But then the past tense switches to the future, Josephine is only about to 'go away'. Soon she will 'joyfully lose herself amid the countless hosts of our heroes' of old. And since this is a nation that has hardly any historical consciousness, her liberation or redemption will be redoubled and heightened—'eine gesteigerte Erlösung': it will be a redemption from the burden of her own life as well as from the perpetuation of that life in the memory of her race. She is no more than 'a little episode in the history of our nation', there are hardly any historians to record that episode: the consolations of artistic immortality are viewed as ironically as is her singing. Perhaps there is a point in the life of an artist where the hope of being read, or listened to, by future generations appears as no more than a last vanity to be conquered. But at that point, too, art comes to an end. Fame, Rilke observed, is no more than a wreath of misunderstandings; posterity, Proust wrote, fashions the artist in its own image. If what Josephine will be remembered by are the silences in which her song and voice were enveloped—the silences which enabled her public to dream their dreams of peace—is that not tantamount to being remembered for a mere nothing, not to be remembered at all?

— J. P. Stern, "Franz Kafka on Mice and Men." *Paths and Labyrinths: Nine Papers from a Kafka Symposium*, ed. by J.P. Stern and J.J. White, (London: University of London Press, 1985): pp. 141-155.

Boris Suchkov on Art's Relevance to Society

[Boris Suchkov was a well-known Marxist literary critic and scholar in Russia during the Soviet era. He is also the author of *The Historical Fate of Realism* and *Images of the Age*. In this essay, he contends that while Kafka reveals that at the end of his own life he began to see art as a distraction unessential to people and society—the story itself disproves Kafka's own conceptions of art and society.]

Josephine, who was endowed with somewhat greater ambition than the common mice, convinced her compatriots that her squeak and squeal were more harmonious than the squeak of ordinary mice who live their stark and difficult lives in a world filled with cares and dangers. Her tenure in the role of servant of the muse was possible only because among the mice there existed something like a private convention recognizing Josephine's particular but, in essence, ephemeral right to be their comforter in times of sorrow or to please them with short hours of joy, which rarely fall to the lot of the mice. Josephine's squeak and squeal grip the imagination of the mice, who on the whole are unmusical by nature and who in the depths of their souls prefer quiet to any music, no matter how good it may be.

With bitter irony, Kafka portrayed the scale of relationships between the artist and society: Josephine allows herself to shock her admirers and even the whole mouse nation; she loves to emphasize her independence from public opinion. But she comes to feel both enmity and malevolence; she feels mistrust of her apparently not very humble trade. At a moment of danger which befalls the mice, she is suddenly filled with a prophetic fever and, straining her whole being, strives to communicate the rapture and alarm which have seized her to her compatriots who do not hear, above the usual noise, the sounds of approaching danger. No, despite all her whims, fancies and oddities, it is impossible to consider Josephine a useless member of society. But the mice had only to doubt her unwritten rights for her career as a free artist to come crashing down and for herself to disappear from the horizons of the hard-working mice and for her memory to fade out of mind.

—Boris Suchkov, "Franz Kafka." *Franz Kafka: An Anthology of Marxist Criticism*, ed. and trans. Kenneth Hughes. (Hanover, NH: University of New England Press, 1981): pp. 125-185.

Ursula R. Mahlendorf on Kafka's Own Creative Process

[Ursula R. Mahlendorf is Professor Emeritus in German and Women's Studies specializing in Expressionism, contemporary German literature, feminist theory and inquiry. She is the author of *The Wellsprings of Literary Creation*, and she edited *Life Guidance Through Literature*. In this essay, she argues that the story not only shows us Kafka's own attempts to deal with the end of his life but also reminds us of the creative process that made Kafka unique.]

The struggle between the narrator and Josephine repeats the pattern of the struggle between Josephine and the mousefolk. In both one of the partners to the struggle is impervious and impassive to the other's struggle; the mousefolk pay no attention to Josephine's struggle; Josephine pays no attention to the narrator's struggle. Due to the resistance each believes they/he encounter from their partners in the struggle, they intensify their efforts. Josephine becomes more dramatic, the narrator becomes more complex and elaborate. However, the concomitant amplification is not based on communication but rather on its absence. It is to remain with the musical image, a spiralling outward of sound waves: as Josephine grows more insistent, the narrator reacts with more resounding defenses. It seems that one drowns out the other, for there is a point beyond which amplification fails. The mousefolk, though they do not know it, lose Josephine; the narrator, though he does not know it, loses Josephine; and Josephine, though she does not know it, loses both mousefolk and narrator. The lack of phasing between the split parts of the self, the reactive quality of the parts in their interaction, the lack of communication, is characteristic of Kafka's art. We might formulate the process in this manner: The omnipresent superego forces of the author's psyche provoke the assault of the id against them and by their impassivity generate an even more intense primary process. The secondary process is stimulated into productivity by the heightened primary process. However, rather than guiding the primary process, rather than defending it to the superego or mediating between it and the superego and de-repressing the affect, the secondary process merely uses partial de-repression as a defense against the primary process and thus reacts to and imitates the primary process. For short times, it becomes as insistent in its argumentativeness as the primary process.

—Ursula R. Mahlendorf, "Kafka's 'Josephine the Singer and the Mousefolk': Art at the Edge of Nothingness." *Modern Austrian Literature: Journal of the International Arthur Schnitzler Research Association* 11 (1978): p. 199-242.

WORKS BY

Franz Kafka

"The Aeroplanes of Brescia" 1909.

"The Judgement" 1912.

"In the Penal Colony" 1914.

"The Metamorphosis" 1915.

"The Bucket Rider" 1917.

"The Hunter Gracchus" 1917.

"The Great Wall of China" 1917.

"Investigations of a Dog" 1922.

"A Hunger Artist" 1922.

"The Burrow" 1923

"Josephine the Singer and the Mousefolk" 1924.

The Trial, published 1925.

The Castle, published 1926.

Amerika published, 1927.

WORKS ABOUT

Franz Kafka

Anderson, Mark. *Kafka's Clothes: Ornament And Aestheticism In The Habsburg Fin De Siècle*. Oxford: Clarendon Press, 1992.

Anz, Thomas. *Franz Kafka*. Originalausg München: C.H. Beck, 1989.

Armstrong, Raymond. *Kafka And Pinter: Shadow-Boxing: The Struggle Between Father And Son*. New York: St. Martin's Press, 1999.

Berkoff, Steven. *Meditations on Metamorphosis*. London: Faber and Faber, 1995.

Boa, Elizabeth. *Kafka: Gender, Class And Race In The Letters And Fictions*. Oxford: Clarendon Press, 1996.

Broyard, Anatole. *Kafka Was The Rage: A Greenwich Village Memoir*. New York: C. Southern Books, 1993.

Corngold, Stanley. *Franz Kafka: The Necessity Of Form*. Ithaca: Cornell University Press, 1988.

Deleuze, Gilles and Félix Guattari. *Kafka: Toward A Minor Literature*; translation by Dana Polan; foreword by Réda Bensmaïa. Minneapolis: University of Minnesota Press, 1986.

Dowden, Stephen D. *Kafka's Castle And The Critical Imagination*. Columbia, SC, USA: Camden House, 1995.

Fickert, Kurt J. End Of A Mission: *Kafka's Search For Truth In His Last Stories*. Columbia, SC: Camden House, 1993.

Gilman, Sander L. *Franz Kafka, the Jewish Patient*. New York: Routledge, 1995.

Glatzer, Nahum Norbert. *The Loves of Franz Kafka*. New York: Schocken Books, 1986.

Goebel, Rolf J. *Constructing China: Kafka's orientalist discourse*. Columbia, SC: Camden House, 1997.

Gray, Richard T. *Constructive Destruction: Kafka's Aphorisms: Literary Tradition And Literary Transformation*. Tübingen: M. Niemeyer, 1987.

Grandin, John M. *Kafka's Prussian Advocate: A Study Of The Influence Of Heinrich Von Kleist On Franz Kafka*. Columbia S.C.: Camden House, 1987.

Greenberg, Valerie D. *Transgressive Readings: The Texts Of Franz Kafka And Max Planck*. Ann Arbor: University of Michigan Press, 1990.

Heidsieck, Arnold. *The Intellectual Contexts Of Kafka's Fiction: Philosophy, Law, Religion*. Columbia, SC: Camden House, 1994.

Janouch, Gustav. *Conversations with Kafka*. Translated from the German by Goronwy Rees with an introduction by Hugh Haughton. London: Quartet Books, 1985.

Jofen, Jean. *The Jewish Mystic in Kafka*. New York: P. Lang, 1987.

Karl, Frederick Robert. *Franz Kafka, Representative Man*. New York: Fromm International Publishing Corp., 1993.

Kempf, Franz R. *Everyone's Darling: Kafka And The Critics Of His Short Fiction*. Columbia, SC, USA: Camden House, 1994.

Kirchberger, Lida. *Franz Kafka's Use Of Law In Fiction: A New Interpretation Of In Der Strafkolonie, Der Prozess, And Das Schloss*. New York: P. Lang, 1986.

Kluback, William. *Franz Kafka: Challenges And Confrontations*. New York: P.Lang, 1993.

Koelb, Clayton. *Kafka's Rhetoric: The Passion Of Reading*. Ithaca: Cornell University Press, 1989.

Kraft, Herbert. *Someone Like K.: Kafka's Novels*. Translated from the German by R.J. Kavanaugh in conjunction with the author. Würzburg: Königshausen & Neumann; Amsterdam: Rodolpi, 1991.

Lawson, Richard H. *Franz Kafka*. New York: Ungar, 1987.

Mailloux, Peter Alden. *A Hesitation Before Birth: The Life Of Franz Kafka*. Newark: University of Delaware Press, 1989.

Mendoza, Ramón G. *Outside Humanity: A Study Of Kafka's Fiction*. Lanham, MD: University Press of America, 1986.

Murray, Jack. *The Landscapes Of Alienation: Ideological Subversion In Kafka, Céline, And Onetti*. Stanford: Stanford University Press, 1991.

Northey, Anthony. *Kafka's Relatives: Their Lives And His Writing.* New Haven: Yale University Press, 1991.

Pawel, Ernst. *The Nightmare Of Reason: A Life Of Franz Kafka.* New York: Vintage Books, 1985, 1984.

Sandbank, Shimon. *After Kafka: the Influence of Kafka's Fiction.* Athens: University of Georgia Press, 1989.

Schur, David. *The Way of Oblivion: Heraclitus and Kafka.* Cambridge: Harvard University Press, 1998.

Spector, Scott. *Prague Territories: National Conflict And Cultural Innovation In Franz Kafka's Fin De Siècle.* Berkeley: University of California Press, 2000.

Speirs, Ronald. *Franz Kafka.* New York: St. Martin's Press, 1997.

Strauss, Walter A. *On The Threshold Of A New Kabbalah: Kafka's Later Tales.* New York: P. Lang, 1988.

Sussman, Henry. *The Trial: Kafka's Unholy Trinity.* New York: Maxwell Macmillan International, 1993.

Tambling, Jeremy. *Lost in the American city: Dickens, James, and Kafka.* New York: Palgrave, 2001.

Thiher, Allen. *Franz Kafka: A Study Of The Short Fiction.* Boston: Twayne Publishers, 1990.

Triffitt, Gregory B. *Kafka's 'Landarzt' Collection: Rhetoric And Interpretation.* New York: P. Lang, 1985.

Whitlark, James. *Behind The Great Wall: A Post-Jungian Approach To Kafkaesque Literature.* Rutherford, N.J.: Fairleigh Dickinson University Press, 1991.

ACKNOWLEDGMENTS

"Samsa and Samsara: Suffering, Death, and Rebirth in 'The Metamorphosis'" by Michael P. Ryan from *German Quarterly* 72 © 1999 by *German Quarterly*. Reprinted by Permission.

"What is it Like to be a Bug?: 'The Metamorphosis' and Marginality" by Mark Sanders from *Journal of the Kafka Society of America* 20 © 1996 by Kafka Society of America. Reprinted by Permission.

"The Narcissistic Drama and the Reader/Text Transformation in Kafka's *Metamorphosis*" by J Brooks Bouson from *Critical Essays on Franz Kafka*, ed. Ruth V. Gross © 1990 by G.K. Hall & Co. Reprinted by Permission.

"Metamorphosis of the Metaphor" by Stanley Corngold from *Franz Kafka's "The Metamorphosis,"* ed. Harold Bloom © 1988 by Chelsea House Publishers. Reprinted by Permission.

"The Dramatic in Kafka's *The Metamorphosis*" by Evelyn Tornton Beck from *Franz Kafka's "The Metamorphosis,"* ed. Harold Bloom © 1988 by Chelsea House Publishers. Reprinted by Permission.

"The Judgment" by Allen Thiher from *Franz Kafka: A Study of Short Fiction* © 1990 by Twayne Publishers. Reprinted by Permission.

"Kafka's 'The Judgment' and Modern Rhetorical Theory" by Stanley Corngold from *Newsletter of the Kafka Society of America* 7 no. 1 © 1983 by Kafka Society of America. Reprinted by Permission.

"Desire's Persecutions in Kafka's 'Judgment,' 'Metamorphosis,' and 'A Country Doctor'" by James McGlathery from *Perspectives on Contemporary Literature* 7 © 1981 by *Perspectives on Contemporary Literature*. Reprinted by Permission.

"Bachelors and Work: Social and Economic Conditions in 'The Judgment,' 'The Metamorphosis,' and *The Trial*" by Bluma Goldstein from *The Kafka Debate: New Perspectives for Our Time*, ed. Angel Flores © 1977 by Gordian Press. Reprinted by Permission.

The Germanic Review, vol. 48, 1973. Reprinted with permission of the Helen Dwight Reid Educational Foundation. Published by Heldref Publications, 1319 Eighteenth St., NW, Washington, DC 20036-1802. Copyright © 1973.

Sternstein, Marlynne. "Laughter, Gesture, and Flesh: Kafka's 'In the Penal Colony.'" *Modernism/Modernity* 8 (2001), 319-320. © The Johns Hopkins University Press. Reprinted by permission of the Johns Hopkins University Press.

"The Ornaments of Writing: 'In the Penal Colony'" by Mark Anderson from *Kafka's Clothes: Ornament and Aestheticism in the Habsburg* Fin de Siècle © 1992 by Oxford University Press. Reprinted by permission of Oxford University Press.

"Kafka's Writing Machine: Metamorphosis in the Penal Colony" by Arnold Weinstein from *Critical Essays on Franz Kafka*, ed. Ruth V. Gross © 1990 by G.K. Hall & Co. Reprinted by Permission.

"'In the Penal Colony'" by Allen Thiher from *Franz Kafka: A Study of Short Fiction* © 1990 by Twayne Publishers. Reprinted by Permission.

Kafka's Rhetoric: The Passion of Reading by Clayton Koelb © 1989 by Cornell University Press. Reprinted by Permission.

End of a Mission: Kafka's Search for Truth in His Last Stories by Kurt Fickert © 1993 by Camden House, Inc. Reprinted by Permission.

"Kafka's 'A Hunger Artist': A Cautionary Tale for Faustian Man Caught Between Creativity and Communion" by Frank Vulpi from *Germanic Notes and Reviews* 24 © 1993 by *Germanic Notes and Reviews*. Reprinted by Permission.

"Kafka and 'The Hunger Artist'" by Breon Mitchell from *Kafka and the Contemporary Critical Performance*, ed. Alan Udoff © 1987 by Indiana University Press. Reprinted by Permission.

Explicator, Vol. 50, 1992. Reprinted with permission of the Helen Dwight Reid Educational Foundation. Published by Heldref Publications, 1319 Eighteenth St., NW, Washington, DC 20036-1802. Copyright © 1992.

"Getting into the Cage: A Note on Kafka's 'A Hunger Artist'" by Joseph M. Garrison from *International Fiction Review* 8 © 1981 by *International Fiction Review*. Reprinted by Permission.

Rickels, Laurence A. "Musicphantoms: 'Uncanned' Conceptions of Music from Josephine the Singer to Mickey Mouse." *SubStance* 58, Vol.18, No.1. © 1989. Reprinted by permission of The University of Wisconsin Press.

The Germanic Review, Vol. 80, 1985. Reprinted with permission of the Helen Dwight Reid Educational Foundation. Published by Heldref Publications, 1319 Eighteenth St., NW, Washington, DC 20036-1802. Copyright © 1985.

"Franz Kafka on Mice and Men" by J.P. Stern from *Nine Papers from a Kafka Symposium*, eds. J.P. Stern and J.J. White © 1985 by University of London Press. Reprinted by Permission.

"Franz Kafka" by Boris Suchkov from *Franz Kafka: An Anthology of Marxist Criticism*, ed. and trans. Kenneth Hughes © 1981 by University of New England Press. Reprinted by Permission.

"Kafka's Josephine the Singer or the Mousefolk: Art at the Edge of Nothingness" by Ursula R. Mahlendorf from *Modern Austrian Literature: Journal of the International Arthur Schnitzler Research Association* 11 © 1978 by *Modern Austrian Literature*. Reprinted by Permission.

INDEX OF

Themes and Ideas